From the author of the best-seller,

dag heward-mills

Aspersions

Fighting accusations

Unless otherwise stated, all Scripture quotations are taken from the King James Version of the Bible.

Excerpts from:

John Wesley - Into All the World by John Telford. Used by permission of Ambassador Publications.

John Wesley by Basil Miller. Used by permission of Bethany House Publishers.

The Spirit-Controlled Woman by Beverly LaHaye. Copyright © 1995 by Harvest House Publishers, Eugene OR. Used by permission. www.harvesthousepublishers.com

DSM-IV-TR Casebook by Spitzer, Gibbon, Skodol and Williams, eds. Reprinted with permission from the Diagnostic and Statistical Manual of Mental Disorders, Fourth Edition, Text Revision, (Copyright 2000). American Psychiatric Association.

Stephen Mansfield, Biography of Derek Prince (Lake Mary, FL: Charisma House, 2005), Used by permission.

E mail Dag Heward-Mills :
bishop@daghewardmills.org
evangelist@daghewardmills.org

Find out more about Dag Heward-Mills at:
www.daghewardmills.org
www.lighthousechapel.org
www.healingjesuscrusade.org

Write to:
Dag Heward-Mills
P.O. Box 114
Korle-Bu
Accra
Ghana

ISBN 13: 978-07963-0840-5

Dedication

To
Emmanuel and Elaine Klufio
Thank you for a great work done in South Africa. You have
built a wonderful church family in South Africa.

Contents

Chapter 1

The Accusers

And I heard a loud voice saying in heaven, Now is come salvation, and strength, and the kingdom of our God, and the power of his Christ: for the ACCUSER of our brethren is cast down, which ACCUSED them before our God day and night.

Revelation 12:10

Although the devil is commonly known as the accuser of the brethren, he is actually the accuser in the midst of the brethren.

In your leadership experience, you will meet different kinds of people. Perhaps one of the most daunting enemies you will ever encounter is "the accuser in the midst of the brethren".

Problems come in different levels but one of the highest problems is to encounter an accuser in the midst of the brethren.

At the highest point of your ministry, you will struggle with the accuser. Accusation is Satan's topmost strategy for dealing with an unconquerable enemy.

Satan's Best Weapon

Satan has different formats by which he operates. He may come to you in the form of a tempter, a liar, a murderer or a deceiver. However, if he takes you on as an accuser, the battle has been lifted to the highest possible level.

This principle is played out in the life of Jesus Christ. Initially, the devil came to him in the form of a tempter. Jesus Christ was tempted in the wilderness for forty days. Satan lied to Him in the wilderness and desperately tried to deceive Him.

Throughout his ministry, the Lord was attacked by the devil in the form of a murderer. "He was a murderer from the beginning" (John 8:44). On several occasions, Satan tried to kill Jesus through mob action but He would escape.

And they got up and drove Him out of the city, and led Him to the brow of the hill on which their city had been built, in order to throw Him down the cliff.

But passing through their midst, He went His way.

Luke 4:29-30, NASB

On another occasion, the devil tried to drown Jesus in the Sea of Galilee but he was not successful because Jesus rebuked the storm. It was not God who brought the storm; otherwise, Jesus rebuked God's wisdom by rebuking the storm.

But as they sailed he fell asleep: and there came down a storm of wind on the lake; and they were filled with water, and were in jeopardy.

And they came to him, and awoke him, saying, Master, master, we perish. Then he arose, and rebuked the wind and the raging of the water: and they ceased, and there was a calm.

Luke 8:23-24

Coming in the Garb of an Accuser

However, Jesus' ministry was finally brought to an end when Satan put on the garb of an accuser. Jesus endured one week of intense accusations, which brought His ministry to an end. This week of intensive accusations, started from Palm Sunday until He was crucified. In Matthew 21:1-17, you will see how He entered Jerusalem triumphantly and cleansed the temple. You will notice how the questions and accusations started from the day after He arrived in Jerusalem (Matthew 21:23).

This time Satan pulled out his deadliest weapon and unleashed it against the Lord. The weapon of accusation was finally deployed. For a whole week before the Passover, the Lord was in the temple being questioned and examined (accused) by the Pharisees.

Then went the Pharisees, and took counsel how they might ENTANGLE HIM in his talk.

And they sent out unto him their disciples with the Herodians, saying, Master, we know that thou art true, and teachest the way of God in truth, neither carest thou for any man: for thou regardest not the person of men.

Tell us therefore, What thinkest thou? Is it lawful to give tribute unto Caesar, or not?

But Jesus perceived their WICKEDNESS, and said, Why TEMPT ye me, ye hypocrites?

Matthew 22:15-18

The Lord was questioned about every aspect of His life and ministry.

For several days, the Lord endured the wickedness and hypocrisy of those who questioned Him in the temple. In the last twenty-four hours of His life, He was also accused in the palace of the high priest, in Pilate's court and also in Herod's palace.

Jesus met this series of high-level accusations with a variety of responses. He answered the temple questions succinctly and made fools out of His accusers.

When they had heard these words, they marvelled, and left him, and went their way.

Matthew 22:22

They had never heard anything like that before.

The officers answered, Never man spake like this man.

John 7:46

However, when in the court of Pilate and other heathen rulers, He answered nothing to the questions that were levelled at Him.

And he answered him to never a word; insomuch that the governor marvelled greatly.

Matthew 27:14

As you can see, Satan has different guises under which he attacks. In this section of the book, we will be dealing with the accusers who are used by the devil to intimidate you. Perhaps you suffer from a plague of accusations in the ministry. Often you do not understand what is happening to you. By the time you finish this book, God will give you wisdom to fight the enemy.

What Is an Accusation?

An accusation is a charge or allegation made against someone. It puts blame and points fingers at a person. An accusation is a statement saying that you think someone is guilty of doing something wrong, especially of committing a crime.

These statements, which are directed at a person, constantly minister a withering and weakening guilt. Only very strong-hearted people can live with persistent accusations for a long time.

Even though accusations come out of human mouths, they are anointed by the accuser of the brethren himself. Satan is the accuser in the midst of the brethren.

Who Are the People Commonly Employed as Accusers?

In my country, some people are commonly employed as security guards. There are also people who are commonly employed as butchers and khebab sellers. Similarly, there are some people whom Satan commonly employs as accusers. These people fall into the category I call "familiar friends" of the accused.

Yea, mine own familiar friend, in whom I trusted, which did eat of my bread, hath lifted up his heel against me.

Psalm 41:9

Familiar friends are the familiar people of your life: friends, husbands, wives, sons, daughters, beloveds, associate pastors, church members, journalists, classmates etc. For accusations to have any impact, they must be channelled through someone close.

Why Not Simply Brush off Accusations?

Are accusations not statements that are true or false? If they are not true, why don't you just ignore them? But it is never as easy as that.

Accusations are anointed from Hell. Accusations are spiritual things. Accusations are tiny arrows loaded with satanic poison. As soon as the poison enters your blood, it spreads through your whole being, attacking your heart. Like some fast-spreading natural poison, you are greatly affected by a seemingly little dart.

I have seen mighty giants of God totally ruffled by unfounded accusations which looked insignificant to the bystander. Such is the power of accusation. It is a puzzling weapon and its effects are mysterious. Truly, accusations are spiritual weapons.

The Pointing of the Finger

Then YOUR LIGHT WILL BREAK OUT LIKE THE DAWN, And your recovery will speedily spring forth; And your righteousness will go before you; The glory of the LORD will be your rear guard.

Then you will call, and the LORD will answer; You will cry, and He will say, "Here I am." IF YOU REMOVE the yoke from your midst, THE POINTING OF THE FINGER and speaking wickedness,

Isaiah 58:8-9, NASB

Accusations are also called "the pointing of the finger". *Such is the evil released by the pointing of the finger, that the light in your life and ministry will actually grow dim from it.* Your light will break forth like the dawn and there will be recovery if you put away the pointing of the finger!

Ministries cannot prosper once a finger-pointing person is allowed to flourish nearby. Much of the darkness in the body of Christ is as a result of the incessant accusations made by brother against brother, sister against sister, husband against wife, and so on.

You must know the people around you who are used to accuse you. Every good leader must understand the principles of accusation. You can wither and weaken in ministry through diverse accusations! Your ministry can actually be misdirected by accusations. I have experienced that myself. Perhaps this is the most important section of this book and I pray you will study it seriously.

The book of Revelation shows how God dealt decisively with the accuser of the brethren. It reveals four amazing benefits of silencing accusations. In these four benefits, we see everything that we desire from God - strength, salvation, power and the kingdom of God. Oh, how much power and strength will be released into your life if the pointing of the finger was not there.

Most ordinary people do not feel that they are qualified to serve God. Most of the people I have trained in the ministry were discouraged and accused by the devil. But I simply encouraged them constantly to serve God and become priests in spite of their shortcomings.

This encouragement was completely contrary to the voice of the accuser in their lives. That voice told them they were not good enough! But my constant encouragement to serve God and to trust Him silenced the voice of the accuser. Suddenly, weak and incapable people received salvation, power and strength to do God's work.

The Benefits of Dealing with the Accuser

And I heard a loud voice saying in heaven, Now is come SALVATION, and STRENGTH, and the KINGDOM OF OUR GOD, and the POWER OF HIS CHRIST: for the accuser of our brethren is cast down, which ACCUSED them before our God day and night.

Revelation 12:10

This Scripture shows four clear blessings of dealing with accusers:

1. Salvation is the first benefit of silencing accusers in your midst.

2. Strength is the next important benefit for eliminating accusers from your little fellowship.

3. The kingdom of our God will come when the accuser of the brethren is cast down.

4. Finally, the power of Christ is released when the accuser is dealt with.

All these benefits are clearly outlined in the Scripture as being things that happen when the accuser is silenced.

If you allow an associate minister to point fingers at you, you will be weakened and the power of God in your life will be reduced. The salvation and the coming of God's kingdom are dependent on you dealing with the accuser.

Chapter 2

The Hidden Laws

Most people do not understand what is happening to them when they are being accused. Because they do not realize what is happening, they play into the hands of the accuser. In this chapter, I want to share some of these hidden laws, which govern the "hows", and "whys" of accusation. Understanding these laws will help you to fight your enemy and gain the upper hand.

Law No. 1

Your Relationships Will Be Polluted by Accusations

Accusations can be likened to the pouring of Satan's faeces or urine on relationships. Accusations can be likened to Satan vomiting on precious relationships.

Somehow, these accusations have the effect of dirtying everything. Pure relationships are poisoned by even the slightest accusations! Nothing is ever the same once you have been accused.

A brother who is accused of having an interest in a particular sister never has a normal relationship with that person anymore. Somehow, that relationship is polluted. He may actually have an interest in someone else. Nevertheless, tension develops in the particular direction of the accusation and everything that was pure looks and feels evil even though it is not! Such is the defiling and polluting power of an accusation.

One pastor described how his pure and undefiled relationship with his church members had been spoiled by his wife accusing him about specific women. He explained, "My wife claims I am interested in certain people. Since then, every time I speak to these people I am supposed to be interested in, I feel sinful. I feel as though I am doing something wrong."

"Nothing is the same anymore," he explained. "Everything has changed and I can no longer work effectively with many people."

"Also, my relationship with my wife has changed. I find myself keeping things from her, which I never used to do. I have to avoid her seeing and knowing certain things so that she will not have missiles with which to fight and accuse me."

He lamented, "I never thought my marriage would degenerate to such a state."

Many pastors poison the relationship between themselves and their associates by accusing them of evils that have not occurred to them. From that time, their relationship is marred and infected with the defilement of accusation. Do not be surprised if one day these people do exactly what they are accused of doing.

I remember a university student who worked in our tapes ministry. He was an honest, hard-working and sacrificial brother who did much to help the ministry. One day, some questions were asked about the finances of the tapes department. In the ensuing discussions, this brother felt he was being accused of stealing. He was shocked because he had sacrificed many things to help the tape ministry.

From that time, our relationship was tainted and it deteriorated until he left the church. I felt very sad about this brother's departure. Since then, anytime there is stocktaking or auditing at the tapes department, I warn them to be very careful about what they say lest they sound accusatory. Accusations will poison beautiful relationships and change them forever.

Rick Joyner, in his vision, described the accusations and condemnations of demons in exactly the same way.

A Terrible Vision of Accusers

Above the prisoners, the sky was black with vultures named Depression.

Occasionally, these would land on the shoulders of a prisoner and would vomit on him. THE VOMIT WAS CONDEMNATION. When the vomit hit a prisoner, he would stand up and march a little straighter for a while, and then slump over, even weaker than before. Again, I wondered why the prisoners did not simply kill these vultures with their swords, which they could have easily done.

As I watched I realized THESE PRISONERS THOUGHT THE VOMIT OF CONDEMNATION WAS TRUTH FROM GOD. Then I understood that these prisoners actually thought they were marching in the army of God! This is why they did not kill the little demons of fear or the vultures - they thought these were God's messengers! The darkness from the cloud of vultures made it so hard for these prisoners to see that THEY HAD NAIVELY ACCEPTED EVERYTHING THAT HAPPENED TO THEM AS BEING FROM THE LORD. They felt that those who stumbled were under God's judgment, which is why they attacked them the way they did - they thought they were helping God.

This book is an attempt to kill the vultures which are vomiting slime on God's servants. It is an attempt to rise up and reject the deception that the slime coming from these vultures is truth from God.

This book is an attempt to reject the notion that many of the accusations we hear are actually true.

It is an open confrontation against accusing women who are destroying their husbands' ministries in the secret places!

It is a rejection of the lies that are peddled about God's anointed through rebellious pastors!

It is a strong stand against the condemnation, news and rumours which look like truth from God!

It is in defiance of the relentless accusations and condemnation meted out to honourable men who have taken up the mantle of service to the King.

Law No. 2

You Will Be Accused of the Exact Opposite of What You Really Are

Amazingly, Satan's strategy is to accuse you of the opposite of what you really are. Many times, ministers labour under the accusations of things they are far from. Men who are as far from being thieves as the sun is from the earth are accused of stealing. Men who will never commit adultery until they die are accused incessantly of being adulterous.

You would have thought that if you accused someone of something remote, it would have no effect on him. Surprisingly these accusations have a powerful effect on the accused.

Moses Was Accused of Being a Murderer

Moses was accused of trying to kill the Israelites even though he was doing the opposite. God had sent him to deliver the Israelites but the people accused him of trying to kill them all. Notice these Scriptures:

And they said unto Moses, BECAUSE THERE WERE
NO GRAVES IN EGYPT, HAST THOU TAKEN US
AWAY TO DIE in the wilderness? wherefore hast thou
dealt thus with us, to carry us forth out of Egypt?

Is not this the word that we did tell thee in Egypt, saying,
Let us alone, that we may serve the Egyptians? For it had
been better for us to serve the Egyptians, than that we
should die in the wilderness.

Exodus 14:11-12

And the children of Israel said unto them, Would to God
we had died by the hand of the LORD in the land of
Egypt, when we sat by the flesh pots, and when we did eat
bread to the full; FOR YE HAVE BROUGHT US FORTH
INTO THIS WILDERNESS, TO KILL THIS WHOLE
ASSEMBLY WITH HUNGER.

Exodus 16:3

And the people thirsted there for water; and the people
murmured against Moses, and said, WHEREFORE IS
THIS THAT THOU HAST BROUGHT US UP OUT OF
EGYPT, TO KILL US AND OUR CHILDREN AND OUR
CATTLE WITH THIRST?

Exodus 17:3

Moses Was Accused of Being Proud

Moses was accused of exalting himself and of being proud.
But the Scriptures tell us that he was the meekest man on earth.

**Now the man Moses was very meek, above all the men
which were upon the face of the earth.**

Numbers 12:3

> **They assembled together against Moses and Aaron, and said to them, "You have gone far enough, for all the congregation are holy, every one of them, and the LORD is in their midst; so WHY DO YOU EXALT YOURSELVES above the assembly of the LORD?"**
>
> **Numbers 16:3, NASB**

Jesus Was Accused of Destroying God's House

Who has done more to build God's house than the Lord Jesus? Who loved the temple so much that He cleansed it of thieves? Who came to earth and sacrificed His life for the house of God? No other person but Jesus Christ! Yet He was accused of planning to attack and break down the temple.

> **WE HEARD HIM SAY, I WILL DESTROY THIS TEMPLE THAT IS MADE WITH HANDS, and within three days I will build another made without hands.**
>
> **Mark 14:58**

The question I ask is, "Did this accusation have the desired effect?" The answer is, "Yes, it did. It worked."

The accusations, even though fantastic and contrary to the known character of the preacher, had the desired effect. Jesus was condemned to death for this accusation. Perhaps your ministry is ending because of baseless accusations. God will work it out by His power like He did for Jesus.

Jesus Was Accused of Wanting Political Power

Jesus was accused of being interested in the throne of Caesar. How far from the truth can we go? Jesus' eyes were on the throne of Heaven, by the heavenly Father.

It is important to recognize that wicked accusations may actually point to the complete innocence of the accused. However, it takes a very seasoned and wise person to recognize what is happening.

And the whole multitude of them arose, and led him unto Pilate.

And they began to accuse him, saying, WE FOUND THIS FELLOW PERVERTING THE NATION, AND FORBIDDING TO GIVE TRIBUTE TO CAESAR, SAYING THAT HE HIMSELF IS CHRIST A KING.

Luke 23:1-2

Jesus Was Accused of Many Different Things

For MANY BARE FALSE WITNESS AGAINST HIM, but their witness agreed not together.

Mark 14:56

And the chief priests ACCUSED HIM OF MANY THINGS: but he answered nothing.

Mark 15:3

Law No. 3

The Most Effective Accusers Are Those Closest to You

Those whose accusations will have the greatest effect are those who are closest to you. The accusations of close people sound credible because of where they have worked. Let me attempt to grade accusations according to the closeness of the accuser.

The accusations of a church member will have more effect than the accusations of a non-church member. The accusations of a general pastor will have less effect than that of a close associate. But the accusations of a wife will carry much more weight than that of any associate.

Even my close friend in whom I trusted, Who ate my bread, Has lifted up his heel against me.

Psalm 41:9

The closer he is, the more credible he sounds. The input of Judas was greater than the input of anyone else because he was a close disciple of Christ.

The Coughing Crabs

One day, somebody told me an interesting proverb. He said, "It is only when you go to the edge of the river that you will hear the crabs coughing."

"What does that mean?" I asked.

He explained, "When you stand afar off and watch crabs running around on the beach you will never know that they actually have a cough. It is only when you are near enough that you will hear them coughing."

He continued, "In other words, it is those who are intimately involved who know what is really going on."

It is therefore such close people who hear the coughing crabs, who are the best accusers.

Crocodile under Water

I also heard somebody say that if a crocodile comes from under the water in the pond and says, "There is a snake under the water", then you must believe him. In other words, it is the crocodile who knows what is going on under the water.

What do all these mean to us? They are warnings for people who work closely with the leader; every close person is a potential future accuser. Friends, close associates, personal assistants, husbands, wives and children are all at risk of becoming accusers. Actually, almost all accusers come from this list. If God has placed you in an honourable position and brought you near, beware lest the accuser uses you to do his work.

Law No. 4

Your Accusations Will Not Stop until You React Wrongly

Moses eventually made a mistake in his ministry. He was under constant pressure from the accusations. Under persistent provocation he disobeyed God. This is the ultimate intention of the accuser: To push you until you change course and falter.

Notice how Moses buckled under the persistent claims that he was a liar and a murderer. Instead of obeying the Lord, he reacted wrongly. He hit the rock with his rod instead of speaking to it. This cost him his ministry and he never saw the promised land.

And there was no water for the congregation: and they gathered themselves together against Moses and against Aaron.

And the people chode with Moses, and spake, saying, Would God that we had died when our brethren died before the LORD!

And why have ye brought up the congregation of the LORD into this wilderness, that we and our cattle should die there?

And wherefore have ye made us to come up out of Egypt, to bring us in unto this evil place? it is no place of seed, or of figs, or of vines, or of pomegranates; neither is there any water to drink.

And Moses and Aaron went from the presence of the assembly unto the door of the tabernacle of the congregation, and they fell upon their faces: and the glory of the LORD appeared unto them.

And the LORD spake unto Moses, saying,

Take the rod, and gather thou the assembly together, thou, and Aaron thy brother, and SPEAK YE UNTO THE ROCK BEFORE THEIR EYES; and it shall give forth his water, and thou shalt bring forth to them water out of the rock: so thou shalt give the congregation and their beasts drink.

And Moses took the rod from before the LORD, as he commanded him.

And Moses and Aaron gathered the congregation together before the rock, and he said unto them, Hear now, ye rebels; must we fetch you water out of this rock?

And MOSES LIFTED UP HIS HAND, AND WITH HIS ROD HE SMOTE THE ROCK TWICE: and the water came out abundantly, and the congregation drank, and their beasts also.

And the LORD spake unto Moses and Aaron, Because ye believed me not, to sanctify me in the eyes of the children of Israel, therefore ye shall not bring this congregation into the land which I have given them.

Numbers 20:2-12

John Wesley came under intense pressure to alter his course of ministry. His wife did not want him to write letters to certain people. She did not want him to carry out his ministry duties of travelling to the churches. But the strong founder refused to alter his ministry.

Married or no, he saw no reason why he should change the course or tenor of his life. He entered in his journal, 'I cannot understand how a Methodist preacher can answer to it to go to preach one sermon or travel one day less in the married than in the single state.'

Law No. 5

The Underlying Causes of Accusation Are the Common Causes of Madness

And the scribes and Pharisees WATCHED him…that they might FIND AN ACCUSATION against him…And they were FILLED WITH MADNESS…

Luke 6:7, 11

Notice how they watched Christ to find something to accuse him of. Eventually, they were filled with madness. Fear and hatred are common causes of accusation.

Men and women full of fear and hatred become the outlet of Satan's accusations. This is another reason why you must keep your heart pure. Keep fear and hatred far from your heart. Let me share with you a little bit of medical science so that you will understand the relationship between accusations and mental illness.

The Causes of Madness

Two cardinal symptoms of madness (schizophrenia) are paranoid delusions and auditory hallucinations. With auditory hallucinations, the patient hears voices accusing him, talking to him and discussing him. With paranoid delusions, the patient is fearful and believes in the existence of things that are not real, and cannot be convinced otherwise.

In mental illness, fears drive the patients down the road of lunacy. In spiritual illness, fears also drive the person down the road of accusations. In mental illness, the fearful state progresses until the patients hear voices and imagine things that are not real.

Do not allow the raging fears of this life to be in your heart. They may drive you towards a mental illness which you never expected. In mental illness the patient believes in things that are not real. With spiritual problems, people are deceived and they cling to their deceptions. It is these deceptions that grow into delusions.

Actually, with the privilege of my medical eye, I have noticed that many apparently normal people are labouring under some form of mental illness. Because mental illness spans a range of behaviour and because there are long periods of lucidity, many of these cases are not picked up.

Many women have succumbed to raging fears and insecurities and have gradually walked the road of mild to moderate psychosis (mental illness). I have actually confirmed the diagnosis of mental illness in many Christians but cannot approach them because they have not sought medical help from me.

Have you noticed that many murderers are filled with passionate hatred for someone? It is this hatred that drives them to do the unthinkable. They knowingly sentence themselves to life imprisonment and hell. This is madness in full manifestation!

The Madness of the Priests

And while he yet spake, lo, Judas, one of the twelve, came, and with him a great multitude with swords and staves, from the chief priests and elders of the people.

Matthew 26:47

The behaviour of the Pharisees and the accusatory priests can best be described as madness. They were filled with such hatred for the Saviour that they did the unthinkable. They "killed" God on a cross. They were so full of fear that they employed Judas to betray someone who walked around openly.

The role of Judas, as a betrayer, is even more mystical when you consider how Jesus openly whipped the temple dwellers a few days earlier.

Their fear of Christ was demonstrated by the kind of army that was sent to arrest one unarmed preacher in a garden.

Then Jesus said unto the chief priests, and captains of the temple, and the elders, which were come to him, Be ye come out, as against a thief, with swords and staves?

When I was daily with you in the temple, ye stretched forth no hands against me: but this is your hour, and the power of darkness.

Luke 22:52-53

Law No. 6

Your Accuser Thrives on Non-Biblical Quotations, Proverbs and Sayings but Not on the Word of God

Accusations thrive on non-biblical quotations and sayings. One day, I received a document from someone who wanted me to believe that my church was a cult-like organization. Initially, I was taken aback by the document, which seemed to be an authority in describing cults.

This document claimed that one characteristic of cults is an emphasis on loyalty. This fellow was therefore pointing out to me that because I have taught on "loyalty" and written books on loyalty, our church has strong characteristics of a cult. These cleverly composed arguments sound true, but can be very misleading. As I studied this paper, I realized that there was absolutely no scriptural backing for these authoritative statements.

Which Bible verse says that when a church teaches on loyalty it is cult-like? Is there not so much in the Bible that teaches us to be faithful? What was the fate of Judas? Did Jesus not say it would have been better that he was not born? About which other sin did Jesus ever say it would have been better that the person was never born? How can the teaching on loyalty and faithfulness to God and His servants be categorized as questionable? Even the suggestion of this is demonic!

The Quips of Women

In addition, other wisecracks have gained prominence and become the basis for wrong behaviour and accusations. In churches, there are unspiritual women living by fear and trumped-up accusations against their husbands and men in general. These women refuse to bend to the Word of God.

They have answers to everything and rely on such statements as:

"It's a woman's world."

"I am a woman and I know what it feels like."

"You are not a woman and you will never understand certain things."

They say things like, "You are men; you are all the same."

"That is how men think."

"Women are made differently."

"You are a man. You have knowledge but no experience of the pain of a woman, etc."

All these clever statements sound reasonable and legitimate. They may be clever but they are not biblical. They must not give strength and foundation to the practice of evil.

We cannot allow the accuser into our midst no matter the garb or costume he wears. He may be all dressed up in pretty dresses and nice hair-dos but it is still the devil!

Law No. 7

When Your Accuser Is Proved Wrong, He Will Follow Up with Several Other Desperate Accusations

Unfortunately, many accusations do not hold water. The accuser is now at risk of being disgraced for making false allegations. This makes him desperate and he resorts to multiple and diverse forms of accusations which become even more bizarre.

The madness builds up as the accuser prosecutes his case and calls in witnesses to confirm that for which he has no proof. Jesus was spat on and buffeted.

Some began to spit at Him, and to blindfold Him, and to beat Him with their fists, and to say to Him, "Prophesy!" And the officers received Him with slaps in the face.

Mark 14:65, NASB

Why did they spit on him? To make him as dirty as they wanted him to be? But our Lord was clean and innocent of all allegations made against Him. Why cover His face and ask Him to prophesy?

They wanted desperately to prove that He was a false prophet. Do not be surprised if your accusers become desperate to find something to use against you.

It is not easy to live with anyone who is searching for a flaw in your life. Since you are a human being, you are likely to slip up at one point or another.

John Wesley said to his wife,

"I dislike the not being safe in my own house. My house is *not* my castle. I cannot call even my study, even my bureau, my own. They are liable to be plundered everyday. You say, 'I plunder you of nothing but papers'. I am not sure of that. How is it possible I should? I miss money too, and he that will steal a pin will steal a pound. But were it so, a scholar's papers are his treasure, my journal in particular. 'But I only took such papers as relate to Sarah Ryan and Sarah Crosby'. That is not true. What are Mr. Landey's letters to them? Besides, you have taken parts of my journal which relate to neither one nor the other."

It is a very uncomfortable feeling to have an accuser as a member of your cabinet or in your home! Jesus did not have it easy. He was under constant scrutiny from people who desperately wanted to find something wrong about Him.

And as he said these things unto them, the scribes and the Pharisees began to urge him vehemently, and to provoke him to speak of many things:

Laying wait for him, and seeking to catch something out of his mouth, that they might accuse him

Luke 11:53-54

Law No. 8

Anyone Associated with You Will Be Accused as Well

Accusations are quickly generalized to include people who associate with you. My assistant pastor is accused of many of the things that I am accused of. If you are not prepared to be collectively accused you cannot be part of the team. Don't expect to be the "Mr. Clean" of the team.

You are not greater than Jesus. If He was accused then you will be too. When similar accusations are levelled at you, it means you are closer to your leader. If Christ was accused of various things, so will you be. If He was accused of destroying the temple, do not be surprised when you are accused of destroying a church. It is an honour to be accused alongside your leader. It is a sign of your closeness. It shows that you have taken up his identity. Thank God for your loyalty.

Peter was accused of being part of Christ's little band. He was the closest and the one who had dared to stay around during the crisis. No wonder the accusations were falling on him as well.

And after a little while another saw him, and said, THOU ART ALSO OF THEM...

Luke 22:58

Another lesson is that it takes a lot to handle certain accusations. Peter's answer to the accusation was to deny it instantly.

...And Peter said, Man, I AM NOT.

Luke 22:58

You must respect men of God who are able to live and minister normally, in spite of numerous allegations and accusations on their life. Peter wilted away at the accusation of a little maid.

Perhaps you would not last a day if you were to experience the accusations of your father! You never know what somebody is going through on your behalf.

Law No. 9

There Are Particular Accusations That Can Push You Around

There are particular accusations that work best on you. Satan will find out what really gets you upset. Then he will hammer on that until you freak out. Pilate refused to crucify the Lord until the worrying voice of the accuser rang above the din of the crowd.

And from thenceforth PILATE SOUGHT TO RELEASE HIM: but the Jews cried out, saying, IF THOU LET THIS MAN GO, THOU ART NOT CAESAR'S FRIEND: whosoever maketh himself a king speaketh against Caesar.

WHEN PILATE THEREFORE HEARD THAT SAYING, HE BROUGHT JESUS FORTH, and sat down in the judgment seat in a place that is called the Pavement, but in the Hebrew, Gabbatha.

John 19:12-13

This voice accused him of not being loyal to Caesar. Pilate was a hard man, known for his brutish behaviour. He was not one to be pushed around by a crowd. But when the accusation came forth, everything changed and he gave up the innocent Christ.

Do you see how powerful accusations are? Accusations can bend the unbendable and push the unyielding leader around. **Satan knows what can push you around! He knows what you hate to hear and he will find somebody to say it to you.**

Are you the one whose mouth is used to speak words of accusation?

Pastors do not like to be called thieves, so when Satan wants to hinder the finances of a ministry, he uses the voice of the accuser to suggest that the pastor is a greedy money-lover. Through this accusation, his hands are weakened and he is unable to raise funds.

Push the Right Buttons, Sister

Pastors' wives know that their husbands loathe being called adulterers. They realize that their husbands do not even want to

26

have that association. Like the Jews who manipulated Pilate to crucify Christ, many Christian wives manipulate their husbands to crucify (eliminate, sack, wipe out, reject, preclude, sweep away and remove) other ladies they dislike or fear! Ladies, sorry for this comparison but it was too appropriate to allow it to pass by. Please do not be angry with me!

Law No. 10

The Motive for Accusation Is Deeper than the Issues Presented

Accusation is a spiritual thing. It is deeper than the issue over which you are being accused. **That is why when you modify your behaviour in response to the accusation, a new set of allegations arise. This is the cardinal sign that the accuser has located you.**

A minister was accused of being involved with drugs. He tried to overcome this cloud that hung over his ministry. He set up drug rehabilitation centres to help drug addicts. This was to prove that he was definitely not into drugs. He did many other good works but the accusations continued.

For as long as I knew this minister, he was constantly bombarded with one thing or another. Public interviews and public relations efforts yielded very little fruit. Why did the journalists never relent in their efforts to accuse this man of God?

One day one of the journalists confessed, "My aim is to make anyone who goes to that church feel ashamed."

What a motive! This man of God was experiencing the unrelenting attack of a journalist because the journalist hated the pastor and wanted to destroy his ministry!

Therefore, every modification this minister made in response to the allegations registered as "no work done". No matter the change in behaviour, a new allegation always springs up. This is the cardinal sign that the accuser has located you.

Satan's intention is to stop you from doing the good works. You will find out that accusations will persist whether or not certain physical things change.

Christ, our Saviour, was a perfect example. His ministry was associated with lunches, parties and breakfast meetings. John the Baptist's ministry was associated with fasting and a life in the wilderness.

But in each case the barrage of accusations intended to stop the ministry continued:

But whereunto shall I liken this generation? It is like unto children sitting in the markets, and calling unto their fellows, And saying, We have piped unto you, and ye have not danced; we have mourned unto you, and ye have not lamented. For John came neither eating nor drinking, and they say, He hath a devil. The Son of man came eating and drinking, and they say, Behold a man gluttonous, and a winebibber, a friend of publicans and sinners. But wisdom is justified of her children.

Matthew 11:16-19

Sometimes there is no need to even think about what you are being accused of. Nothing you do will change anything. The problem is not what you are doing. The problem is with the accuser. Notice this interesting testimony by Beverly LaHaye in her book *"The Spirit-Controlled Woman"* which demonstrates this same principle.

Another hang-up common to Martha Melancholy is jealousy. Not given to "insincere flirtation" Martha often marries a man who is outgoing and friendly to everyone. **It is not uncommon for her to ride home in icy silence after a party because her husband flirted with every woman there.** Since her husband's male ego gets so little food at home, he unwisely seeks it at social gatherings and he may often think, "Nothing I do ever satisfies that woman."

Seated across from the beautiful wife of a wealthy and dynamic Christian businessman, I was startled to hear his melancholic wife asking, **"Would you explain why I am so jealous of my husband even when I know I have no reason for it?" It seems that he had dismissed three successive secretaries and finally hired the homeliest gal he could find because of his wife's jealousy. But it still didn't solve her problem.**

I responded, "The problem is not with your husband; you just don't like yourself." Tears ran down her cheeks as she admitted to strong feelings of rejection.

Later, her husband commented on their love life: "When her groundless suspicions make her jealous, I can't touch her. **But when she is sorry for her accusations, she can't get enough of me. I never know whether to expect feast or famine!"**

Chapter 3

The Aims of the Accuser

There are mysterious purposes for accusing someone. These hidden intentions are not known to most Christians. If you understood what accusations do, you would be very hesitant to accuse anyone. Accusations destroy people. Accusations destroy relationships between people. The effects of these accusations are often permanent.

First Purpose of Accusations: To Degrade the Accused Person

Accusations degrade you in your own eyes. Accusations make the accused person have a low estimation of himself. You therefore lose the zeal to do well. The zeal to be good or to remain a good person goes after you have heard certain accusations.

You say to yourself, "After all, they are not expecting anything good from me. I will just be myself. I do not care anymore."

Once you are degraded, you are good for nothing. You are not useful for any great mission.

This is where fathers come in. Fathers believe in their children even when they are sacked from school. They love their children even if they are pregnant out of wedlock. They constantly say good things to their children.

"I believe in you! You can make it!" It is these words which counteract the degradation that is imposed on the accused person, and give him power to rise up again.

I remember when I began our church, I was accused of several things. I was told, "You have no business entering the ministry. You are not a pastor! You are a medical student and nothing more."

My own associate pastor questioned my calling. My associates and church members would have discussions to analyze my preaching and my calling. Some said, "He is not called by God." Others said, "He is called."

I became so frightened of the church that I would have a running stomach on Saturday nights. I asked my beloved (fiancée) whether I would have diarrhoea every Saturday for the rest of my life.

I was so scared to preach on Sundays. My critics and accusers would line up and sit on the second row to assess my calling. My hands would shake as I held the microphone. I experienced tremors as though I was suffering from Parkinson's disease.

Whilst I preached, one look at their faces was enough to dry up my mouth. There would be no more saliva in my mouth and I would need to drink water desperately to moisten my mouth, otherwise my tongue could no longer move within my mouth. Sometimes, someone would have to get water for me urgently during the sermon and I was also accused of being interested in the girl who would give me water!

One day, I had a vision and saw myself in a boxing ring, boxing away against an opponent. I suddenly realized who I was fighting with - a prominent lady and church member.

The Lord revealed to me that this person and some others were fighting against me with their tongues.

He said to me, "Cast out the scorner and strife and contention will go away." I did exactly that and dismissed the leader of my accusers. He went out of the church and most of the accusers left as well. After getting rid of the accusers, I became stronger. This is what the Bible teaches. Strength comes when you cast away accusers!

I did not become a more anointed or experienced pastor immediately. But I did become stronger by not having them around me! Those accusations could have driven me out of the ministry as they were intended to. I would never have written this book and you would never have benefited from this ministry.

Second Purpose of Accusations: To Disgrace You

Accusations also disgrace the accused in the sight of others. Satan wants to disgrace you through accusations. Have you not noticed that when someone is accused of a crime and has to defend himself, he is usually disgraced?

Defending yourself in court is usually a disgraceful experience. You are never the same after the accusations have come and gone. Somehow people believe that the accusations were true. They think you escaped on technicalities.

Michael Jackson was accused of child molestation. He went to court for several weeks. Even though he was acquitted of all these charges, he is not the same person. The shine and the glimmer have dimmed.

As your reputation is blackened, people cannot receive from you. Your ministry is prevented from spreading. Fewer and fewer people want to listen to you. They believe you are an evil person. "As many as received Him, He gave power." In order to receive the power, you must receive the person. If the person is blackened, and made out to be evil, how can you receive him?

I remember a man of God who experienced unrelenting accusations from his own wife. She was obsessed with the possibility of him having affairs with several women in the church. One day, God gave him a vision in which He revealed that the man of God was being attacked by a spirit of disgrace. In this vision, he found himself in the toilet like every other person, and attending to a call of nature. It happened that whilst still attending to this call of nature, he had a distinguished visitor whom he respected very much.

Surprisingly, his wife brought the visitor to the toilet to see him. The whole room smelled terribly as it does for everyone else and her husband was very embarrassed. He asked for the visitor to be made to wait elsewhere. But his wife insisted that the person stand just outside the toilet and speak to him from there. This poor husband had to speak from behind the door to the honourable guest who was made to stand in the terribly smelling area.

In the vision, the husband was so embarrassed by this experience. When he woke up, he realized that he was encountering a spirit of disgrace in his life, which wanted to embarrass him for no evil done.

I also remember years ago when a great evangelist had planned a crusade for Ghana. His forerunner was in the country and stayed in a hotel that my father owned. One of the pastors of our city came in to meet this crusade director. Unfortunately, this Ghanaian pastor spent a long time blackening the reputation of one of the seasoned ministers of the city. As we passed by, we heard snippets of their conversation.

For every second that went by, the reputation of this senior pastor was blackened with soot from this other pastor's mouth. From the kind of things that were said about him, he would only look like a spiritual golliwog!

The aim of accusations is to ensure that you will never be received. But God will ensure that you are received at the places where you must be received. Your ministry cannot be hindered by any human being. God is above everything and He will bring His will to pass in spite of all that is said about you.

Third Purpose of Accusations: To Make You Fall into Sin

After being accused and degraded, many develop a low esteem and actually begin to do the things people (the accusers) expect of them.

For as he thinketh in his heart, so is he...

Proverbs 23:7

Satan's clever plan now begins to work. You find yourself doing the evil that was spoken about you. This is why experienced people do not even to bother to listen to certain accusations. It is not that they are arrogant but these things tend to push you towards an intended target.

I remember counselling a pastor who was married to an accusatory and insecure woman. This pastor told me tearfully how his wife constantly suspected him of having affairs with ladies in the church.

He said to me, "I love my wife and I am not having an affair with anyone." For years, their marriage continued swinging through the highs and the lows created by one accusation after another.

The pastor narrated how, one day, his wife was approached by someone who had a vision that her husband had an affair with someone in the church. With tears in his eyes, he told me that his wife believed the lady wholeheartedly and actually arranged a meeting with the visionary for him to discuss her vision of his adulterous affair. The pastor told me how he was totally embarrassed by this encounter. He lamented, "How could my wife believe this vision and actually arrange the meeting? She does not believe nor trust me."

34

One day, I said to the wife, "If your husband ever has an affair with anyone I would blame you. You have done the work of Satan and accused him, suspected him and disgraced him for years." I also said to her, "If your husband does ever have an affair, my love and respect for him will not change. He has withstood your withering accusations for years and I do not even know how he has survived." She did not seem to understand what I was saying. I continued, "Because you have accused him for so long, it would be your greatest victory for him to actually sleep with someone. This would vindicate you and prove that you have been right all along."

This is a common but amazing reality. The accuser actually wishes that the accusations come true so that she would be proved right in the eyes of the people she has made her claims to. Eventually, after many years, this pastor did end up having a sexual encounter with a lady who was not even one of the suspected persons.

The pastor explained to me: "I was so low. I felt my wife did not love me and that she actually hated me. This drove me into the arms of this lady who was welcoming and kind to me."

Naturally, this pastor was devastated and his ministry was greatly affected. I felt sorry for this minister because he had fallen prey to a clever, sustained, long-term strategy of the devil. Dear friend, watch out for accusations. They are having an effect that you cannot imagine. The Scripture teaches that accusations weaken you and take away your power. It is time to silence the accuser. No one can flourish in the presence of accusers.

Fourth Purpose of Accusations: To Generate Hatred and Bitterness in the Accused

Satan's aim is to induce a spirit of hatred in your heart. Once you are full of bitterness many other evils will grow. It is natural to hate your accusers. It takes supernatural grace to love your accusers. Every minister experiences this temptation. Once there is hatred and unforgiveness in your heart, a door is opened through which Satan will bring disease, death and other difficulties.

Many ministers have hatred within them for someone. Usually they have not forgiven someone for things said against them. This person may be an associate, a church member or even a journalist. But this is just a trap to push you into unforgiveness. I have seen ministers trembling with hatred for church members who departed with a string of accusations. Don't forget that Satan wants to fill your heart with bitterness. It is a long-term strategy of the devil to finish you off.

Fifth Purpose of Accusations: To Bring about Separation

One of the purposes of accusations is to separate the accuser and the accused. Usually it is important for the accuser to be close to the accused.

For instance, a senior pastor and his assistant can be separated through accusations.

A husband and a wife easily move apart and become distant when one person constantly accuses the other of various things. Husbands and wives grow further and further apart as they accuse each other of various deficiencies through the years. Before they married, they praised each other and bestowed words of love on each other.

Positive words bring people closer, negative accusations separate even the closest of friends!

Churches are divided into groups through accusation. The Ashanti tribe is separated from the Ewe tribe through various accusations that they fling at each other. The divide only gets deeper and wider as the accusations increase.

Sixth Purpose of Accusations: To Discourage and Confuse You

So I will incite Egyptians against Egyptians; And they will each fight against his brother and each against his neighbor, City against city and kingdom against kingdom.

Then the spirit of the Egyptians will be DEMORALIZED within them; And I will CONFOUND [CONFUSE] their strategy...

Isaiah 19:2-3, NASB

The Scripture above shows how when a brother attacks another brother it demoralizes and confuses their front. The Egyptians would become confused because of the kinds of attacks they would get.

When you are accused, you become discouraged and disillusioned. Accusations have the power to take the life and spirit out of you. When all your good deeds are seen in a negative light your zeal is dampened.

Years ago, one of my best friends and brothers was living with his auntie. One day, something was stolen from their house and the auntie accused him of stealing the things. He had lived happily with this auntie and her family for many years. He was shocked that he was being accused of stealing. His few possessions were searched and he was threatened greatly by his auntie and uncle.

However, he had not stolen anything. It was actually someone else who had stolen the items. Eventually, it was proved that he did not steal the things. But he told me his relationship with his auntie and her entire household was never the same after that. It is not a nice feeling that someone should think of you as a thief. Discouragement and now separation had set in. Close important relationships were destroyed by accusations.

Seventh Purpose of Accusations: To Turn a Friend into an Enemy

So I will incite Egyptians against Egyptians; And they will each fight against his brother and each against his neighbor, City against city and kingdom against kingdom.

Then the spirit of the Egyptians will be DEMORALIZED within them; And I will CONFOUND [CONFUSE] their strategy,

Isaiah 19:2-3, NASB

When Satan wants to turn good brothers against each other, he uses his weapon of accusation. Accusation has the mysterious effect of turning best friends against each other. Husbands and wives who came together through deep love and affection can turn into enemies. It is an amazing thing to watch how a relationship deteriorates into the opposite of what it was at the beginning.

Churches would have been a hundred times bigger if there were no accusations. Junior pastors level accusations against the senior pastor and leave the church with a section of the membership. Many churches have a breakaway church situated somewhere nearby. These two churches are usually led by pastors who used to be friends, but now are enemies. This enmity was created by accusations. Satan is the author of all these things.

God wants us to be one body. Let us recognize the accuser in our midst and refuse to be used to accuse one another.

Abner Turned against Ishbosheth

An example of how good friends are turned into enemies was when Abner turned against his own king. Abner had established and supported Ishbosheth to be the king of Israel. He did this faithfully and fought wars against king David. One day, something happened that changed all this. Ishbosheth accused

Abner of wrongfully relating with a lady. Abner was so upset about this accusation that it turned him against the king. He quickly undid all that he had done for Ishbosheth and became his enemy. It was an amazing turnaround. Read it for yourself.

Now Saul had a concubine whose name was Rizpah, the daughter of Aiah; and Ish-bosheth said to Abner, "Why have you gone in to my father's concubine?"

Then Abner was very angry over the words of Ish-bosheth and said, "Am I a dog's head that belongs to Judah? Today I show kindness to the house of Saul your father, to his brothers and to his friends, and have not delivered you into the hands of David; and yet today you charge me with a guilt concerning the woman.

"May God do so to Abner, and more also, if as the LORD has sworn to David, I do not accomplish this for him, to transfer the kingdom from the house of Saul and to establish the throne of David over Israel and over Judah, from Dan even to Beersheba."

And he could no longer answer Abner a word, because he was afraid of him.

2 Samuel 3:7-11, NASB

Do you want to turn your best friend into an enemy? Then go ahead and accuse him. Do you want your husband to hate you and become your enemy? Then I suggest that you begin to accuse him. Ask Ishbosheth what happened to him and you will receive wisdom.

Do you want to lose your associate pastor? Then accuse him instead of encouraging him.

This is why I encourage people even though I can see their faults. In the midst of much love and encouragement, it is easy to address faults and deal with them without the bitterness of accusation.

I am able to correct and rebuke those that work with me on almost anything. I do this gently and very sparingly after making sure that the message of love is louder and clearer than anything else.

I spoke to a lady who was constantly accusing her husband of having an affair with someone. This brother had not done any of the things she was claiming. As the months went by, she maintained her unproved allegations. She would not budge or relent. "My husband is committing adultery," she insisted.

She could not see that she was turning her own husband into an enemy. In a desperate attempt to gain the love of her husband, she was pushing him further away and actually making him hate her. Her own husband turned into an enemy. I watched as that couple walked down the road of increasing separation and hatred for each other.

Countless women practise this form of accusatory love. "Accusatory love" sends out accusations that are intended to frighten the husband away from other women and to draw him to her. Unfortunately, this type of love has the opposite effect and actually makes the husbands hate their wives.

Eighth Purpose of Accusations: To Turn You into an Accuser Yourself

When you are accused, you often become an accuser yourself. You often rise in self-defence to protect yourself from the onslaught. This is a dangerous development. Every minister should watch out for this. Not only have you developed bitterness, hatred and enmity, but you are now putting on the garb of an accuser. You and Satan now join forces and work together as partners. Perhaps this is the most deadly development in the response to accusations.

To see this clearly, you only have to observe human behaviour in politics. The opposition or minority groups come up with numerous accusations and allegations against the ruling party.

The president and his ruling party respond vehemently with counter-accusations about unrelated issues. Parliament is basically a theatre for accusations and counter- accusations. It is an arena where hatred is generated and existing divisions are deepened. No one sees the good in the other; meanwhile each is as bad as the other.

Ninth Purpose of Accusations: To Stop You in Your Tracks

Satan desires to stop you from doing the good works God has called you to. One of the most effective ways is to find something to accuse you of.

After planting several churches in Europe, I was accused of so many different evils. Years of hearing negative things eventually took their toll on me. I lost interest in Europe and did not want to plant churches there anymore.

No More Church Planting

One time, I was in a particular city in Switzerland. A group of people who wanted us to start a church there had gathered to meet with me. As they spoke earnestly of their desire to have a church in the city, I looked at them suspiciously.

I thought to myself, "These very people will turn against me and accuse me of coming here to hunt for money."

I mused, "They are the same as the other accusers in those European cities. It is just a matter of time before they point the finger at me."

I decided not to start the church there. "They don't deserve it," I concluded.

Later on, I realized that I had stopped church planting because of accusations. When Satan wants to stop you, he has one weapon that works - accusation, accusation, accusation! It will stop you in your tracks!

My Girlfriend?

Some time ago, I was the leader of a fellowship. I had many members who were scattered all over the city. When we were in school, I would see all my members and care for them. However, during the holidays I had to visit them to minister to them. One day, I was visiting a particular sister at a small shop where she worked for her auntie.

As I entered the shop, I heard someone whisper behind the counter, "Your boyfriend is here."

I was taken aback because I was not her boyfriend, and I had no intention of becoming her boyfriend. After hearing that comment, it was difficult to minister to the girl. I lost interest in following her up and decided to stop visiting and ministering to her. You see, that comment was an accusation that led me to stop my ministry to this needy soul. The effect it had on me was to stop me from doing my good work. I left her to her fate! Evil spirits took over and eventually she became possessed with demons. The last time I heard of her, her life was destroyed and she had gone mad!

Satan wanted access to my sheep and he wanted me to stop being a shepherd. He simply used his weapon of accusation and it was good enough! I was stopped in my tracks by a simple accusation.

Tenth Purpose of Accusations: To Control You

Accusations can stop you but they can also control you. They become a basis for decisions you take. Eventually, you will find yourself on a course completely different from what God intended for you. Years ago, the Lord led me to begin a fellowship of ministers in my city.

I was concerned about what some people would say and think about me. I heard people say, *"Who does he think he is? He is a small boy! When did he come on the scene? Does he think he is going to rule over us?"*

I felt very bad and ended up forming a democratic group to please them. Interestingly, none of the people whose comments and accusations I was responding to ever joined the fellowship, even though I had made it democratic for their sakes.

Later on, I found myself unable to fulfil the commission God had given me. I realized that the comments and accusations of people had guided my decisions concerning that fellowship. I had been controlled by these insinuations and accusations until my ministry was stifled.

Some people are called to be pastors but do not want to be associated with the priestly profession. This is because they have heard numerous accusations against ministers and would not like to be one of them. This keeps many well-meaning people out of the ministry. Through effective accusations, Satan keeps the number of ministers as low as he can.

Witchcraft through Accusations

This is how witchcraft develops. Witchcraft is the use of any power other than the power of God to control people. Sadly, the only biblical examples I have are examples of women moving their husbands against the will of God.

Eve moved the hand of Adam to pluck the fruit of the tree of the knowledge of good and evil. Since then we have been struggling on earth to make ends meet. To make things worse, we are all in danger of going to Hell! If it had not been for the mercies of God, we would all be condemned.

Jezebel moved the hand of her husband, Ahab, to kill an innocent man. Through her influence, the king joined a long list of evil kings and murderers on their way to Hell.

Herod's wife moved the hand of her husband to kill (eliminate, delete, preclude, reject, wipe out, remove, obliterate) the ministry of the prophet, John the Baptist.

One way of establishing control is to accuse and pester someone with words. You control someone when you accuse them of what they would not want to be. People tend to recognize what you would not want to be and accuse you of being exactly that.

Each accusation gets you heated and angry. Through persistent accusations, controlling people stop you from doing certain things, which they do not like.

As someone continues to accuse you, he achieves a level of control over your life and this is witchcraft. This kind of witchcraft is not easy to recognize. It is only after a long time that you may recognize that you are being controlled. Sometimes those accusing you do not know that they have moved into the realm of witchcraft!

It takes a very strong spiritual person to maintain his course in spite of accusations. Lesser men are unable to hold their course. Sometimes they react by simply snuffing out the accuser.

Strong Men Withstand Accusations

John Wesley is an example of a man whose wife tried to control his life. She accused him endlessly of having affairs with different women who were writing to him and serving him. She knew that John Wesley, being who he was, would utterly dislike and even fear to be so described. Although these accusations may seem natural, or even legitimate, it is important to diagnose witchcraft when it is manifesting.

One day, John Wesley, founder of the Methodist Church, wrote a letter to his wife. His very words reveal the passion with which he asked to be free from the controlling power of his wife through accusations. He begged his wife to allow him to be controlled by God and by his conscience.

John Wesley's Letter to His Wife

"I love you still, and am as clear from other women as the day I was born. At length know me and know yourself. Your enemy I cannot be. But let me be your friend; suspect me no more; asperse me no more; provoke me no more. Do not any

longer contend for mastery; for power, money or praise. Be content to be a private insignificant person, known and loved by God and me. ATTEMPT NO MORE TO ABRIDGE ME OF THE LIBERTY, WHICH I CLAIM BY GOD AND MAN. LEAVE ME TO BE GOVERNED BY GOD AND MY OWN CONSCIENCE; then shall I govern you with gentle sway, and shew that I do indeed love you, even as Christ the church."

Obviously, God and our consciences are better guides than the raging jealousy and hatred of a woman. John Wesley never left his marriage. He remained married to the same person in spite of the withering accusations he suffered. This is true Christian virtue played out to its fullest and I honour him for that.

Weaker Men Wither under Accusations

Weaker men do not respond so well to this sort of treatment. I remember a brother who got married and lived happily with his wife for several years. After many years, this couple was not able to have a child. After a while, several stormy situations arose and the brother decided to divorce his wife. It was an unfortunate turn of events.

One day, this brother released a bombshell. He said, "I did not leave my wife because we did not have a child. I left her because I could no longer take the accusations." She would constantly accuse me of having affairs with one person or another. She thought I was trying to have a child outside the marriage."

He described how there were times she would accuse him of having affairs with people he did not even know. She even accused him of having an affair with a bystander at a bus stop whom he had never spoken to in his life.

Accusations separate couples and this couple was separated by incessant accusations. The more she accused him, the more they separated. And the more they separated, the more she accused him. The day came when he broke away.

This is not a good reason for divorce. I am just giving this example to illustrate how different people respond to

45

accusations. John Wesley weathered the accusations and understood what was happening to him. But lesser people do not weather the storm; they wither away from the onslaught that greets them on a daily basis.

Eleventh Purpose of Accusations: To Induce Fear

Satan wants you to be filled with fear. Fear is an evil spirit which is a *forerunner spirit* and the *way-maker spirit* for other unclean devils. When your mind is filled with fear, it usually makes a way for other evils. That is why fear is a *way-maker* and a *forerunner spirit*.

One day, a senior minister told me something his wife had said. He had had an argument with her about various things. She warned him to change his ways. She said, "You go on and have affairs with those girls. You will lose your ministry!" This was a pastor of a large church.

Fear gripped his heart and he thought to himself, "Lose my ministry?" Mercy!

The thought of all the possibilities raced through his mind and he became more fearful. Once the spirit of fear is in you, other spirits can have access to you. Perhaps, one day, you will say, "What I feared greatly has come upon me."

Do not allow fear to make a way for other stronger demons to enter your life.

Twelfth Purpose of Accusations: To Weaken the Minister

Accusations reduce self-confidence and self-esteem. This weakens the hand of the accused. One day, a pastor decided to have a three-day miracle convention. The power of God flowed and he ministered to the congregation with signs and wonders.

When he got home after the second night of powerful ministrations, his wife summoned him for a meeting.

She said, "During the ministration time, I was not happy with the way you were laying hands on certain people."

"It seemed that you were laying hands on some particular girls longer than others," she added.

The brother was taken aback, "What?" he stuttered.

"Which girls were these?" he asked.

The brother explained, "There was no such intention and I do not understand what you are talking about."

Anyway, the next day, he had to continue his miracle service. When it was time for laying on of hands, he did not know what to do. When he felt the spirit leading him to pray for some people, he would think of his wife and how she was keeping a close eye on him.

He was so intimidated that he was hardly able to minister to anyone. He mumbled a few words and closed the service. Such is the power of accusation - to weaken and to remove self-confidence from strong men.

Another brother who had a very good reputation in the church had this sorrowful tale to tell. When he got married, his wife began to accuse him of being interested in other church members.

She did not want him to relate with certain people. One time, as his custom was, he went dancing in front of the church with a group of other Christians. He had done this several times but now she claimed he was dancing closer to certain sisters. She was convinced about her evidence. She believed that he was interested in the dancing girls.

With weepy and tearful eyes, she spoke about the pain her husband was causing her due to his dancing. "My heart is in pain," she moaned. "I am a woman and I know what I see. I would not say such things unless there was a good reason!"

This dear brother could no longer dance in church. Every dance and every move now had an evil connotation.

Thirteenth Purpose of Accusations: To Deceive You

Faith comes by hearing and hearing by the Word of God. After hearing something for a while, it is difficult to disbelieve it. People tend to believe what they hear, no matter how absurd it sounds. *Accusations will make you believe that you are a bad person when you are actually a good person.* The devil will tell you that bad people are not welcome at certain places. He will ask you to go away from the company of the saints and other good people. Satan will try to keep you away from the places God has called you to.

Persistent harassment with accusations can lead to a good person becoming convinced that he is bad. In medical science, there is something called *folie a deux* which means "the madness of two". A good example of *folie a deux* is the story of this couple in which the husband accused the wife until she believed that she was what she was being accused of. She actually believed that she was doing something that she was *not* doing.

In a particular case, the husband complained that his wife had had many extramarital affairs, with many different men, all through their married life. He insisted that in one two-week period she had had as many as a hundred different sexual experiences with men outside the marriage.

His wife herself agreed with his assessment of her behaviour, but would not speak of her experiences, saying that she "blocks" the memories of the adultery out. She denied any particular interest in sexuality, but said that apparently, she felt a compulsive drive to go out and seek sexual activity despite her lack of interest.

The patient had been married to her husband for about twenty years. He was clearly the dominant partner in the marriage. The patient was fearful of his frequent jealous rages, and apparently, it was he who suggested that she enter the hospital in order to receive hypnosis.

The patient maintained that she could not explain why she sought out other men; that she really did not want to do this. Her husband stated that on occasion, he tracked her down, and when he had found her, she acted as if she did not know him. She confirmed this and believed that it was because the episodes of her sexual promiscuity were blotted out by "amnesia".

When the physician indicated that he questioned the reality of the wife's sexual adventures, the husband became furious and accused the doctor and the ward attendant of having sexual relations with her.

Extensive counselling was not able to bring out the memory of periods of sexual activities. The patient did admit to a memory of having had two extramarital relationships in the past: one twenty years before the time of admission and the other just a year before the admission. She stated that the last one had actually been planned by her husband and that he was in the same house at the time. She continued to believe that she had actually had countless extramarital sexual experiences, though she remembered only two of them.

It was diagnosed by psychiatrists that the husband, the chief informant, had delusional jealousy, believing that his wife was repeatedly unfaithful to him. *Apparently, under his influence, his wife had accepted this delusional belief explaining her lack of memory of the events by believing that she had "amnesia".*

Because her delusional system developed as a result of her close relationship with another person who had an already established delusion (i.e. her husband), and because her delusions were similar in content with his delusions, the diagnosis is Shared Psychotic Disorder traditionally known as *folie à deux*.

As you can see, the madness is shared by both the accuser and the accused. This true story illustrates the concept of accusations leading to deception. Faith comes by hearing. There comes a time you must silence the accuser and not allow yourself to hear the rubbish talk of the enemy about you. Be careful lest you believe things that are not true. Pastor, do not believe the lies and accusations that are spoken about you. You are a good person. You are an honoured servant of the Lord. Even the fact that you have attempted to serve the Lord makes you an honourable person.

Fourteenth Purpose of Accusations: To Stereotype You

A stereotype is a fixed pattern or picture that occurs without variation. Through accusation, Satan creates a picture which he claims will not vary, *even in your case*. For instance, there may be a stereotype that all artisans are liars. Therefore when you become an artisan, it is a natural inference that you must be a liar.

Another example of a stereotype is that all pastors have affairs with their church members. Another stereotype is that all bosses have affairs with their secretaries. Another stereotype is that all politicians are thieves and liars. Yet another stereotype is that all stepmothers are wicked.

When you come along, Satan's goal is to stereotype you. All he has to say is that you are this kind of stereotype. As soon as that stereotype is associated with you, you find it difficult to shake off that picture.

When you become a pastor, you will constantly battle with the stereotype that you must be a man who has affairs with his church members.

If you become a secretary, you will constantly battle with the stereotype that you must be a woman who has affairs with her bosses.

If you ever become a stepmother, you will battle the stereotype that you must be a wicked and heartless woman who has no love or pity for her stepchildren.

Fifteenth Purpose of Accusations: To Destroy Relationships

Another name for the "accuser *of the* brethren" is the "accuser *in the midst of the* brethren". Satan loves to enter our sweet fellowship and get us to accuse one another.

Suddenly, the cordial relationship is broken and everyone is against the other. Watch out for people who point out something bad in everyone! The spirit of the accuser is upon them. Accusations create mistrust between lovers. Suspicion sets in and everyone gets ready for battle.

A classic example is found when the relationship between King David and the Ammonites changed from friendship to enmity. David had an excellent relationship with the Ammonites and intended it to continue that way. He sent a message of condolence with a very good intention, to the new king of Ammon. Unfortunately, the new king interpreted this gesture wrongly and accused David of spying. This accusation brought about the end of all the good relations between the two nations.

Whenever a good intention is misinterpreted and accusations are exchanged, love turns into hatred. *Millions of relationships have gone sour through this cycle of good intentions being rewarded with accusations.*

This is what is called the David-Hanun syndrome.

How Best Friends Become Enemies
The David-Hanun Syndrome

Now it happened afterwards that the king of the Ammonites died, and Hanun his son became king in his place.

Then David said, "I will show kindness to Hanun the son of Nahash, just as his father showed kindness to me."

So David sent some of his servants TO CONSOLE HIM concerning his father. But when David's servants came to the land of the Ammonites, the princes of the Ammonites said to Hanun their lord, "DO YOU THINK THAT DAVID IS HONORING YOUR FATHER because he has sent consolers to you? Has David not sent his servants to you in order to search the city, to spy it out and overthrow IT?"

So Hanun took David's servants and shaved off half of their beards, and cut off their garments in the middle as far as their hips, and sent them away.

When they told it to David, he sent to meet them, for the men were greatly humiliated. And the king said, "Stay at Jericho until your beards grow, and then return."

Now when the sons of Ammon saw that they had become odious to David, the sons of Ammon sent and hired the Arameans of Beth-rehob and the Arameans of Zobah, 20,000 foot soldiers, and the king of Maacah with 1,000 men, and the men of Tob with 12,000 men.

When David heard of it, he sent Joab and all the army, the mighty men.

The sons of Ammon came out and drew up in battle array at the entrance of the city, while the Arameans of Zobah and of Rehob and the men of Tob and Maacah were by themselves in the field.

Now when Joab saw that the battle was set against him in front and in the rear, he selected from all the choice men of Israel, and arrayed them against the Arameans.

2 Samuel 10:1-9, NASB

Pastors who have good intentions for their congregations are shattered when they hear wicked accusations about themselves.

for whom they had such good intentions, suspect them of trying to harm them. Relationships quickly deteriorate and accusations are exchanged. This is how the David-Hanun syndrome is repeated.

Church Divides into Little Pieces

I remember a denomination whose founder died tragically. There was much sorrow as all the junior pastors who had worked under their overseer mourned. The funeral was a big event and thousands of people attended.

These pastors had worked together for years under their Bishop. As time went on, the pastors decided to establish a foundation to support the family of the dead overseer.

After thousands of dollars were raised for the founder's family, the records of the foundation were kept secret from another section of the pastors. Somehow, they felt that those pastors could not be trusted with the details.

This is when the accusations began. One group accused the other of keeping the records secret so they could steal from them. Another group accused the other of deeming them too insignificant to be told what was going on. Yet another group said they had no right to keep the information secret in the first place.

Even though everyone started out with good intentions to provide support for the founder's family, the accuser in the midst of the brethren divided and scattered everyone. The pastors only had good intentions as they tried to set up this founder's trust. As people tried to protect the money and ensure its proper use, accusations only heightened and increased. Needless to say, this denomination began to break up into different groups.

Today, the entire denomination is fragmented and scattered into little bits and pieces. This is the work of the accuser in the midst of the brethren. Churches are divided, husbands are set against wives, and wives against their husbands. Women's groups against men's groups! Church members postured against their pastors and pastors are set against other pastors. The David-Hanun syndrome is working fully in churches, families, businesses and homes. Meanwhile, everybody has a good intention and everyone means well. No one understands why there is no "flow" and no unity.

Can the Accuser Divide a Threefold Cord?

...and a threefold cord is not quickly broken.

Ecclesiastes 4:12

I remember a church, which was run by a strong leader with two equally strong and gifted assistants. The leadership of this church was a great example of a threefold cord. These three ministers held the fort in a spectacular fashion: preaching, teaching and leading worship in tandem and setting a wonderful example of partnership and teamwork. Many church leaders admired the success of this anointed trio.

They seemed to have all the keys for fruitfulness, largeness and effectiveness in ministry.

They used the key of the two witnesses: By the word of two or more witnesses a thing is established (Matthew 18:16). When the leader would preach a controversial message, the other assistants would speak on the same theme but use a different Scripture and sermon title. This equally strong message resounded through the church and their words were established. Indeed, their sermons were like the oracles of God. Even those who were not a part of their church were affected by whatever they said.

They used the key of common love: They were together and had all things in common (Acts 2:44). This trio related as brothers and their families related closely. When one of them would have a baby, the others would go to the hospital and get involved with all the goings on.

One day, I was chatting with one of them and he said to me, "Some people think they can divide us, but we cannot be divided."

He continued, "They don't know how close the three of us are. Do you know what we talk about? We share everything and we even talk about our private sex lives with one another."

He laughed disparagingly at people who made any attempt to divide their powerful team.

They used the key of unity: How pleasant it is for brethren to dwell together in unity (Psalm 133). This trio was united in all respects.

One day, a member of this powerful leadership trio visited me at home. As we chatted, he told me about how an enemy pastor of their church had tried to divide them.

He said, "This guy always wants to meet my senior pastor without the two of us. He is forever trying to meet him and say things to him on the side. He is jealous of the unity we have."

"Really", I answered. "Why would he do something like that?"

He continued, "You won't believe what he said the other day."

I remember exactly where he sat as he narrated his tale.

He said, "This fellow had the audacity to tell my senior pastor that God had given him a revelation."

"What was the revelation," I asked.

He answered, "He told my senior pastor that he had seen him in the spirit with two 'Goliaths'. One 'Goliath' was standing on his right and one on his left."

"What were these 'Goliaths' doing?" I asked.

"He said God had shown him that these two 'Goliaths' would attack him one day and try to take over the church!"

"Amazing," I mused. "Two 'Goliaths' trying to take over the church?"

"So who are these two 'Goliaths'?" I asked.

"We are the 'Goliaths!' Myself and the other associate. Can you believe it? He is calling us 'Goliaths'! And he is saying that we are going to take over the church."

This pastor found it preposterous that anyone could imagine them ever being divided. Who could separate this ideal partnership of two perfect assistants?

But Satan watches every united team closely, hoping for a chance to become the accuser in the midst of the brethren. He does not think any team is impregnable! He does not consider any group untouchable!

Just a few years after this incident, the perfect trio began to disintegrate right before our very eyes.

They hurled railing accusations at one another. The "accuser in the midst of the brethren" had penetrated their ranks. After months of bitter allegations and counter-accusations, the perfect trio parted company and went their separate ways.

Chapter 4

Employees of the Accuser

S atan would like to talk to us directly. He would like to say how bad we are and describe our sins to us as vividly as possible. Fortunately, he does not have that chance because we are operating in different realms. Satan is a spirit operating in the spirit realm and we are human beings operating in a physical realm.

Accusations are very effective, and Satan relies heavily on them. He, therefore, needs workers to carry his foul and degrading messages. Satan knows he can weaken, degrade, deceive and even control God's servants through accusations. Satan desperately needs workers he can employ as his mouthpiece. He will rain foul, slimy faeces on God's holy men through these workers. Do not become the mouthpiece of Satan.

Satan wants to defecate and vomit on God's servants. Will you be the tool of Satan from which he will spray good people with his defiling accusations?

Never Accept Satan's Job Offer

Do not accept this job from the devil. Accusations are the trademark of the devil. I want you to learn a lesson from the angel Gabriel who refused to accuse even Satan. Why would Gabriel not want to accuse someone who is a confirmed, certified, evil being? Because that is not the way of God. As soon as you begin to accuse someone, you have taken over from Satan and done the work of a demon!

Yet Michael the archangel, when contending with the devil he disputed about the body of Moses, durst not bring against him a railing accusation, but said, The Lord rebuke thee.

Jude 9

If even an angel would not accuse Satan, why would you choose to accuse someone as good as your pastor? Why would you accuse your husband or your wife? Can the evil in your husband or your wife be compared to the evil that is in Satan? Then why do you accuse them? Pray for them and love them.

God is the only One who can change a human being! You will not bring about a positive change in someone by accusing him. He may be pushed around for a while by your accusations but one day he will rebel.

"No more," he will say. "I will choose my own way from now on." That is what John Wesley said in a letter to his wife. *"Attempt no more to abridge me of the liberty, which I claim by God and man. Leave me to be governed by God and my own conscience..."*

Who will be the mouthpiece of Satan and do the work of demons? Not everyone can do this work of accusing people. Some people are more suitable than others are. Some people are actually predisposed to this finger-pointing ministry! Let me give you some examples of the type of people predisposed to becoming accusers.

The List of Potential Accusers

1. Evil men: It is said that it takes a thief to catch another thief. Usually, evil people know how the evil mind works. Innocent people do not have the slightest idea about many possible evils. It is when you are corrupted that certain ideas even occur to you.

Sometimes, I hear people accusing others of things, which I find absurd. "How could they think of such a thing", I ask.

Yet, some of these accusations are proved to be realities. Many times these ideas come to people from experience. You see, when you have used your office to steal millions of dollars before, you will know that large amounts of money can be stolen by politicians. You will not find it unusual to suggest that someone would steal such monies.

Is it not interesting that it was Judas, the thief, who pointed a finger at Christ for not caring for the poor? This is the way to know the evil men in your midst. They seem to spot evil and accuse quickly because they themselves are evil.

> **Then saith one of his disciples, Judas Iscariot, Simon's son, which should betray him,**
>
> **Why was not this ointment sold for three hundred pence, and given to the poor?**
>
> **This he said, not that he cared for the poor; but because he was a thief, and had the bag, and bare what was put therein.**
>
> **John 12:4-6**

2. Bitter and unforgiving people: These people have suffered many hurts and pain. They therefore trust no one and expect no good thing from anyone.

Some people who come out of bad relationships become the wildest accusers of their future partners. They have no trust.

Because African leaders have looted the treasuries of their nations, Africans generally do not trust their leaders. The best of leaders are met with numerous accusations about their lives. It is difficult to lead an army of suspicious and accusing people.

> **Moreover David was greatly distressed because the people spoke of stoning him, for all the people were embittered, each one because of his sons and his daughters. But David strengthened himself in the LORD his God.**
>
> **1 Samuel 30:6, NASB**

Notice how David's men thought of stoning (attacking) David. These men were hurting and grieving men. They were ripe and ready to become accusers.

3. Insecure and jealous people: People who are not secure in their positions tend to attack anything that comes around them.

An insecure female dog, which has littered, will attack anyone who comes near her puppies. She feels a threat to the lives of herself and her children.

Insecure senior pastors attack their associates and accuse them of disloyalty and unfaithfulness.

Insecure husbands and wives constantly accuse their spouses of having an interest in other parties. Often, the husband or wife is jealous of how their partner seems happy in the company of others. This generates jealousy and insecurity.

An insecure head of state constantly fears being overthrown. He is constantly spying on people and accusing those around him. He may execute some members of his government from time to time to discourage mutinous ideas from growing.

One pastor was transferred and for the first time had the job of heading the church and relating with all sorts of people. One day, his wife freaked out and accused him of being in love with the worship leader. This pastor was so shocked at the accusation that he almost had a fit. But his wife would not relent.

Unexpectedly, she asked him, "Tell me, are you in love with her?" She continued, "Come on, do you love her? I need an answer now!"

Her husband was bewildered but she continued with her confrontation.

She said, "You should see the way you look at her!"

She hammered on, "You should hear your voice on the phone when you are talking to her."

One day, she said to him, "I know you are having an affair with a married woman and you know what I am talking about."

She was convinced that he was in love with her. Sadly, this outburst marked a major downturn in this minister's marriage. All the negative effects of accusation played out in the marriage, which had hitherto been peaceful.

This is how insecurity becomes a problem for marital couples. In the ministry, honourable men are sometimes accused in private by their insecure wives. I do not blame you if you do not understand these examples.

The Pharisees were insecure because Jesus had a huge following. They sought to destroy him because He threatened their very existence. The hypocrisies of the Pharisees were exposed by Christ. Even Pilate could see through their insecurities and jealous accusations.

But Pilate answered them, saying, Will ye that I release unto you the King of the Jews?

For he knew that the chief priests had delivered him for envy.

Mark 15:9-10

4. Fearful people: A good example of an accusatory person is the servant who was given one talent. He accused his master of being hard and of reaping what he did not sow.

However, the root of these accusations was revealed when he said, "I WAS AFRAID and I hid the talent in the ground." His fearful spirit made him attack his master with accusations.

Then he which had received the one talent came and said, Lord, I knew thee that thou art an hard man, reaping where thou hast not sown, and gathering where thou hast not strawed:

And I WAS AFRAID, and went and hid thy talent in the earth: lo, there thou hast that is thine.

Matthew 25:24-25

These are people who harbour the spirit of fear. Such people are fearful of many possible evils. They are constantly expecting the worst thing to happen. Such people tend to accuse those around them of something very bad. They may accuse their best and most honest workers of stealing. They may accuse their husbands or wives of having affairs. The great fears they have in their hearts are manifested through accusations.

5. Men of hatred: "But this cometh to pass, that the word might be fulfilled that is written in their law, they hated me without a cause" (John 15:25).

Accusations are manifestations of hatred. Satan uses people who hate you to accuse you. Your accuser is the one who hates you most. The hatred that politicians have for one another is manifest through the accusations they hurl at each other. *Please do not say you love someone whom you accuse! You do not love him!* You hate him because you hate the one you accuse!

6. Witches: A person with a controlling spirit is a witch. Accusations harass and threaten God's servants. Accusations are perfect tools to control great people.

A witch is someone who has realized that she has this power to twiddle people around her thumb. She controls people and makes them do things they would not have done. She wields this power through relentless accusations.

A minister complained that he no longer felt free in his home. Witchcraft had modified his domestic behaviour! He told me how he had to always hide his phone from his wife who would search through the phone for incriminating text messsages and evidence of questionable phone calls.

In the end, he became a fugitive in his own house, running to answer calls in private and rushing about to ensure that his phone was not available for inspection.

This controlling witchcraft had converted a normal husband into a strangely-behaving man who lived on tenter-hooks in his own home. One day, a friend living with him noticed the tension surrounding his handling of the phone and asked, "What is wrong with you?"

He said, "My wife charges me with various allegations. The other night she accused me of being interested in someone.

She confronted me and said, 'Can't you leave that girl alone?'

She continued her barrage, 'You speak to her first thing when you wake up and she is the last person you talk to before you go to bed'."

He lamented, "I have no such interest and God knows my heart. I have never had anything to do with any lady and God knows my heart."

This lady was trying to control her husband's life, relationships, and even his use of his phone. Through horrible-sounding accusations, she tried to deter him from calling or speaking to people. It takes a strong person to see through these accusations and not be confused.

Jezebel sent a frightening message to Elijah about how she was going to kill him. This was a form of accusation. Elijah was under threat for the lives of the four hundred prophets of Baal who had perished under his ministry.

Jezebel, the named "witch" in the Bible, harassed the man of God in her day.

> **Then Jezebel sent a messenger unto Elijah, saying, So let the gods do to me, and more also, if I make not thy life as the life of one of them by to morrow about this time.**
>
> **1 Kings 19:2**

She controlled her husband with her words and her actions.

> **Jezebel his wife said, "IS THIS HOW YOU ACT AS KING OVER ISRAEL? Get up and eat! Cheer up. I'll get you the vineyard of Naboth the Jezreelite."**
>
> **Kings 21:7, NIV**

7. Ungrateful people: People who are not thankful for what they have received often have little restraint when attacking loved ones.

"I don't owe you anything," they say. The Israelites accused Moses of trying to kill them. They were not grateful to him for delivering them from Egypt. If you were thankful for the privileges that have come to you through certain people, you would never want your mouth to be used to rain slime, vomitus and faeces on them.

In my experience, I find that accusers are often ungrateful people with short memories; they do not understand how God was good to them through certain people.

For example, they wanted to stone Jesus (a physical form of accusation) without cause.

> **Jesus answered them, Many good works have I shewed you from my Father; for which of those works do ye stone me?**
>
> **John 10:32**

8. Forgetful people: The children of Israel forgot how they had suffered as slaves. They forgot the experience of passing through the Red Sea. They forgot how the armies of Pharaoh had drowned in the Red Sea. They forgot how bitter waters had been sweetened by Moses. They forgot the manna that came from

Heaven. They forgot about the pillar of cloud by day and the pillar of fire by night. They forgot how much gold they had carried out of Egypt. And so they complained and accused Moses of numerous unbelievable crimes including, evil intentions, murder and genocide (killing entire groups of people).

THEY FORGAT God their saviour, which had done great things in Egypt;

Wondrous works in the land of Ham, and terrible things by the Red sea.

Therefore he said that he would destroy them, had not Moses his chosen stood before him in the breach, to turn away his wrath, lest he should destroy them.

Yea, they despised the pleasant land, they believed not his word: BUT MURMURED in their tents, and hearkened not unto the voice of the LORD.

Psalms 106:21-25

9. Hard-hearted people: People with hardened hearts cannot believe in the grace of God.

They do not trust in the love of God. They cannot forgive. They cannot believe there is any good thing in someone who has made a mistake. They cannot receive counsel. They cannot stop attacking fathers, pastors and authority figures. Their hearts are hardened. These are perfect vessels meet for the devil's use as accusers.

10. A person with a melancholic temperament: "...If you remove the yoke from your midst, THE POINTING OF THE FINGER and speaking wickedness" (Isaiah 58:9, NASB).

Melancholics are perfectionists. It is easy for them to feel that people have stepped out of line. They have their own laws of life and expect people to measure up to their standards. With such a personality it is easy to see wrong in many things and point them

65

out. The pointing out of people's weaknesses often becomes full-blown accusations. Be careful that you do not become the finger-pointing member of the church.

11. A person with a phlegmatic temperament: Phlegmatic people are perceived as good, calm people who stay out of trouble. A phlegmatic person, not affected by the Word is usually a very lazy person.

These phlegmatic Christians are therefore often self-righteous people - perfect in their own eyes. Such people quickly notice when others fall short. They can become judgemental and accusatory.

The servant who accused the master of being harsh was actually *a slow-moving and lazy person,* perhaps a phlegmatic man.

His lord answered and said unto him, Thou wicked and SLOTHFUL servant, thou knewest that I reap where I sowed not, and gather where I have not strawed:

Matthew 25:26

12. Disloyal people: Often, when someone turns against his father without justification, he becomes an accuser. He often needs to justify himself to others for the stand he has taken.

Ministers who turned against me without a cause have often railed strings of accusations against me. I have a long list of different things I have been accused of. I have been accused of almost every evil under the sun. Watch out for disloyal men! They are top-class accusers employed by Satan to poison the church.

Absalom, the disloyal son who tried to kill his father, accused him to outsiders. He accused his father of neglecting the kingdom and mismanaging affairs.

And Absalom rose up early, and stood beside the way of the gate: and it was so, that when any man that had a controversy came to the king for judgment, then Absalom

called unto him, and said, Of what city art thou? And he said, Thy servant is of one of the tribes of Israel.

And Absalom said unto him, See, thy matters are good and right; but there is no man deputed of the king to hear thee.

Absalom said moreover, Oh that I were made judge in the land, that every man which hath any suit or cause might come unto me, and I would do him justice!

2 Samuel 15:2-4

13. Your enemies: Accusation is the language of your enemy. I detect the presence of an enemy by any hint of suspicion or accusation.

In parliament, enemy parties accuse one another of different evils because they are political enemies.

When husbands and wives are not lovers but enemies, they accuse one another of even imaginary things. Do not think that you love your wife if you accuse her! You do not love your husband if you accuse him of different things. Accusation is the language of an enemy and not a friend.

I am amazed that ministers love to be interviewed by journalists who accuse them of a variety of evils. They do not perceive that they are sitting with an enemy. You can never justify yourself to your enemy. He hates you and wants to see you destroyed.

Jesus did not bother to respond to interviews with evil men. He could speak for hours to His disciples, but when He was in the presence of accusers, clothed in the garb of justice, He clamped up and said nothing.

And while He was being accused by the chief priests and elders, He did not answer.

Then Pilate said to Him, "Do You not hear how many things they testify against You?"

67

And *He did not answer him with regard to even a single charge,* so the governor was quite amazed.

Matthew 27:12-14, NASB

14. People with something to cover up: Often people cover up their own sin by being the first to attack! They take the battle to the enemy's gate by being the first to strike. Watch the accusers very well. They are often evil men with many things to hide. The author of accusation is the devil. God does not accuse anyone. This means that he who is truly righteous and holy, does not accuse.

Is it not ironical that Ahab would accuse Elijah of troubling Israel? Who was causing more trouble in Israel than Ahab? And yet this very person had the audacity to accuse Elijah of troubling Israel.

And it came to pass, when Ahab saw Elijah, that Ahab said unto him, Art thou he that troubleth Israel?

And he answered, I HAVE NOT troubled Israel; BUT THOU, and thy father's house, in that ye have forsaken the commandments of the LORD, and thou hast followed Baalim.

1 Kings 18:17-18

15. Mentally unwell people: Mentally unstable people suffer from delusions. One of the cardinal symptoms of madness is delusions.

When a person has a delusion, he believes things that are not true in spite of evidence to the contrary. He often accuses the other party of various crimes, which are not real. Watch every accuser closely. He or she may be suffering from a mental problem that needs medical attention.

Chapter 5

Accusing Women

E very man of God has different devils and problems to contend with. Some men of God have to deal with powerful, accusing women who have the capacity to stop them in their tracks.

Unfortunately, this topic is rarely spoken about because few men of God would ever reveal what they experience in the privacy of their homes. After all, every pastor is supposed to have a happy marriage and a blissful existence with his beautiful, well-chosen spouse.

There are rare moments when a man of God speaks about his personal difficulties and experiences. Besides these rare glimpses, there is virtually no insight to the challenges that some ministers do encounter.

It is therefore necessary to read between the lines and to receive instruction and encouragement from others who are experiencing similar temptations.

God's servants must open their eyes to see and their ears to hear. As Isaiah stated, many of God's servants are blind and deaf. They simply cannot interpret the veiled messages that are given by God's men.

> **Who is blind but My servant, or so deaf as My messenger whom I send? Who is so blind as he that is at peace with Me, Or so blind as the servant of the LORD?**
>
> **You have seen many things, but you do not observe them; Your ears are open, but none hears.**
>
> **Isaiah 42:19-20, NASB**

Challenging Our Favourite Men

Job

Many of our favourite people in the Bible were challenged by accusing women. We do have some glimpses, which reveal the challenges that some of our favourite men encountered. Most of these men reacted decisively against evil coming to them through women.   Job, for instance, was pushed towards damnation by his wife. Listen to her:

> **Then said his wife unto him, Dost thou still retain thine integrity? curse God, and die.**
>
> **Job 2:9**

But Job reacted instantly and rebuked his wife. He would serve God and have none of her foolishness. He said to his wife:

> **...You speak as one of the foolish women speaks. Shall we indeed accept good from God and not accept adversity? In all this Job did not sin with his lips.**
>
> **Job 2:10, NASB**

Moses

Another of our favourite men was Moses. You would have thought that Moses would enjoy a smooth ride as he led the people of God with many miracles. But Miriam, his sister, was not impressed. She rose up with an accusing tongue and charged him for marrying the wrong person.

And Miriam and Aaron spake against Moses because of the Ethiopian woman whom he had married: for he had married an Ethiopian woman.

Numbers 12:1

She was not impressed by Moses' success at the Red Sea nor was she impressed by his achievements in the wilderness. She took him on squarely and challenged him about his private life. Moses trembled at the accusations of Miriam. But God intervened and struck her with leprosy. God did not seem to be bothered by what Miriam was complaining about. It is what God says that matters. No matter what issue your wife or any woman may bring up, never forget that she is *not* God and she is *not* a god! God is still God and it is His opinion that matters.

…wherefore then were ye not afraid to speak against my servant Moses?

And the anger of the LORD was kindled against them; and he departed.

Numbers 12:8-9

David

King David had won great victories in various battles. But his wife, Michal was not impressed by what impressed outsiders. She knew David too well to be taken in by the crowds that sang his praises. She knew David had killed Goliath, but it did not matter. She knew David was anointed but she was not impressed.

All she thought of was how David was undressed in front of the giggling girls of the congregation.

Then David returned to bless his household. And Michal the daughter of Saul came out to meet David, and said, How glorious was the king of Israel to day, who uncovered himself to day in the eyes of the handmaids of his servants, as one of the vain fellows shamelessly uncovereth himself!

2 Samuel 6:20

But David responded decisively. He disagreed with Michal. "I was not displaying in front of those church girls! I refuse to accept that comment! I cannot accept this kind of talk in my house! Do not re-describe my worship as undressing in front of little girls who are enamoured with me! My mind was on God and is still on God!" And that was the end of Michal!

And that would also be the end of many wives of ministers of the Gospel if the ministers would respond that decisively to accusations.

David was so angry that he said he would continue dancing and playing before the Lord: "I will do more and I will go as far as I want to!" He said, "I have my freedom to serve God and I refuse to be controlled by you. You are not God and I will not obey you! I will obey God whom I love!" Can you imagine if David had been restrained in his worship? What would have happened if he had followed the warped and narrow-minded prescriptions of Michal?

And David said unto Michal, It was before the LORD, which chose me before thy father, and before all his house, to appoint me ruler over the people of the LORD, over Israel: therefore will I play before the LORD.

And I will yet be more vile than thus, and will be base in mine own sight: and of the maidservants which thou hast spoken of, of them shall I be had in honour.

Therefore Michal the daughter of Saul had no child unto the day of her death.

2 Samuel 6:21-23

Elijah and John the Baptist

Elijah had a long-standing conflict with King Ahab. After a while, he found out that he was actually dealing with a woman called Jezebel. She was the witch who was fighting him from behind the scenes. Naboth also found out that he was fighting with Jezebel and not her husband, Ahab. Naboth actually lost his life because of Jezebel's involvement in the vineyard case.

Jezebel his wife said to him, "Do you now reign over Israel? Arise, eat bread, and let your heart be joyful; I will give you the vineyard of Naboth the Jezreelite."

1 Kings 21:7, NASB

After manipulating Ahab from behind the scenes, she threatened Elijah openly and directly.

Then Jezebel sent a messenger unto Elijah, saying, So let the gods do to me, and more also, if I make not thy life as the life of one of them by to morrow about this time.

1 Kings 19:2

Stages to Becoming a Jezebel

Women do not become Jezebels overnight. They go through seven stages, which they must recognize if they are to deal with this tendency. A spiritual woman is able to detect, admit and confess these tendencies before they override all her Christian virtues.

Stage 1:   **Involves women having what I call flashes of annoyance at the sight or presence of certain people.**

This is a kind of unexplained displeasure or even discomfort when the person comes around. When such a person enters you are no more at ease.

Stage 2: Is a state in which the woman does not want the presence of certain people.

These people should not be close by. They should not be in any environment or place where they are; be it home, work, church, small group, etc. In stage two, the woman takes active measures to avoid being together with or near the other person. If she has any power she would use it to ensure the other person is kept out of sight.

Stage 3: This is when the lady has nothing positive to say about another woman.

She sees nothing good or positive in the other person. For instance, someone may say, "The lady sang very well!"

But the lady in stage three will say that the instrumentalists are the ones who made the song nice. Another instance is where someone may comment on the beauty of the newsreader but the person in stage three would chip in that it is the free costumes and the make-up artists that make the newsreader look nice!

Someone may also say, "That lady has been promoted because of her hard work." But the stage three lady would be sure to counteract that the boss likes her and that is why she seems to be doing well. Somehow, no positive comment comes forth from a person in stage three about another lady.

Stage 4: This is when negative remarks are made about the undesirable person.

Initially, there was nothing positive to say, but now there are a lot of negative things to remark about. Complaints about the other person's behaviour and attitude are often given. The displeasure and dislike are now fully expressed!

Stage 5:   **This is when there are clashes between the women: unexplained confrontations, conflicts and quarrels.**

There is no end to the discord between these ladies. Often, there is not much explanation to the clashes and the continuation of conflict seems to be unavoidable.

Each one blames the other lady for a bad attitude. They also blame each other for failing to speak or share openly about certain things because of the other party's evil mind. Usually, both ladies would claim that they have good relations with everybody else and that they are not the type that quarrels with anyone. This, each uses as proof that there is nothing wrong with her but the main problem is the witch in the other lady. Sometimes the clashes take on the form of silence and extra-reservedness.

Stage 6:   **This is the stage of hatred and elimination.**

One lady would like to get rid of the other and use all her powers to do so. If she has the power, she would eliminate, terminate and delete the undesirable person. In some cases murder even occurs. This stage of elimination explains the frequent turnover with domestic helpers who work more directly with the women.

Stage 7:   **This is the stage of delusions.**

A woman who has progressed through these stages without any restraint from the Word of God moves dangerously towards delusions, madness and the arbitrary use of every power she has. Such a person is full of accusations about the other party and cannot be convinced about anything contrary to her beliefs.

Fighting Him in Secret

Powerful women, suffering from delusions, are able to fight against the greatest anointings that have ever walked the earth. What greater anointing is there than the anointing of Elijah or John the Baptist? Yet, Jezebel and her New Testament sister, Herod's wife, fought against God's anointed servants. Jezebel and her spiritual sister, Herod's wife, are classic examples of fully deluded women who live out the evil within them. They followed their delusions to their logical conclusions.

These powerful women have a secret, which they deploy against God's servants.

The secret of these powerful, accusing women is that they take on these anointed men in secret and when they are alone.

Elijah was informed that he was the only person in Israel who was to die within the next twenty-four hours. Can you imagine how he felt? The entire government machinery had been marshalled to eliminate one humble prophet who had a home in the desert.

Elijah was terrified and he ran for his dear life! Jezebel was more powerful than all the four hundred false prophets put together. She put Elijah to flight. Elijah had to call on any cross-country or marathon experience that he had to save his life. Even his servant could not keep up with his speed and abandoned him in Beersheba.

This is exactly what happened to John the Baptist as a result of the scheming by Herod's wife. He was alone in the prison cell when he heard the sound of marching feet. There appeared two men with a big tray and the sharpest knife in Israel.

Underground and all alone, he screamed and shouted, "What a contradiction this is. I have done no evil. I have only helped to restore morality and to reduce corruption in the city."

But they would have none of that. After all, they were alone with John the Baptist. There was nothing he could do and no one could help him in this secluded and secret place. They sawed off his head, slowly cutting through the neck muscles, his trachea, the carotid arteries and finally separating the cervical vertebrae until John the Baptist was well and truly decapitated. What a messy scene was created, as the blood of John the Baptist squirted out from his headless body onto his clothes, and on the Scriptures he had been reading; in preparation for his next sermon, which he had hoped to deliver in two weeks' time!

This man of God was attacked alone where no one could be called upon to help him! No one would understand what was happening to John the Baptist. Everyone in town was happy and there was a party going on upstairs in the castle. There was singing and dancing because it was the king's daughter's birthday. No one would understand or relate with John the Baptist's problems on such a festive occasion. That is how it is with men of God. No one really understands what happens to them underground and in the secret places where few ever venture.

Jesus said there was no greater man born of woman than John the Baptist. And yet a woman had taken him on in secret and destroyed him. Dear minister, you are not greater than John the Baptist or Elijah. These stories are to encourage you to fight on and to understand that greater people than yourself have struggled in ministry against the power of accusing and threatening women.

Unfortunately, not all of them survived. But we console ourselves that the will of God always comes to pass. I love a Scripture, which gives me the assurance that God's will is what happens at the end of the day.

The LORD of hosts has sworn saying, "Surely, just as I have intended so it has happened, and just as I have planned so it will stand,

Isaiah 14:24, NASB

John Wesley in the Dungeon?

John Wesley was the great founder and leader of the Methodist church. His life and ministry was plagued by the problem of an accusatory and threatening woman. Of course, he would never say so because the problem was personal. He encountered his problem all alone in the privacy of his room. He suffered the confusion that besets a man of God who needs to love his belligerent wife and yet fulfil his ministry.

He had no comment or book that we know of in which he spoke of his problems. However, a glimpse into the dungeon is given to us by a long letter that he wrote to his wife. It is revealing, and every sentence of this letter is a summary of the dungeon experience. His wife was called Molly and this is a letter he wrote to her.

Coleford October 23rd, 1759

Dear Molly,

I will tell you simply and plainly the things which I dislike. If you remove them, well. If not, I am but where I was.

1. I dislike your showing any one of my letters and private papers without my leave. This never did any good yet, either to you or me or anyone. It only sharpens and embitters your own spirit. And the same effect it naturally has upon others. The same it would have upon me but that (by the grace of God) I do not think of it. It can do no good. It can never bring me nearer, though it may drive me further off. And should you do as you often threaten me, then the matter is over. I know what I have to do. In all this you are fighting against yourself. You are frustrating your own purpose if you want me to love you. You take just the wrong way. No one ever was forced to love another. It cannot be: love can only be won by softness; foul means avail nothing. But you say, 'I have tried fair means and they did not succeed'. If they do not, none will. Then you have only to say, 'this evil is of the Lord; I am clay in his hand.'

2. I dislike not having the command of my own house, not being at liberty to invite even my nearest relation so much as to drink a dish of tea without disobliging you.

3. I dislike the being myself a prisoner in my own house, the having my chamber door watched continually, so that no person can go in or out but such as have your good leave.

4. I dislike the being but a prisoner at large even when I go abroad, inasmuch as you are highly disgusted if I do not give you an account of every place I go to and every person with whom I converse.

5. I dislike the not being safe in my own house. My house is not my castle. I cannot call even my study, even my bureau, my own. They are liable to be plundered everyday. You say, "I plunder you of nothing but papers". I am not sure of that. How is it possible I should? I miss money too, and he that will steal a pin will steal a pound. But were it so, a scholar's papers are his treasure, my journal in particular. 'But I only took such papers as relate to Sarah Ryan and Sarah Crosby'. That is not true. What are Mr. Landey's letters to them? Besides, you have taken parts of my journal which relate to neither one nor the other.

6. I dislike your treatment of my servants (though, indeed, they are not properly mine). You do all that in you lies to make their lives a burden to them. You browbeat, harass, rate them like dogs, make them afraid to speak to me. You treat them with such haughtiness, sternness, sourness, surliness, ill-nature, as never were known in any house of mine for near a dozen years. You forget even good breeding, and use such coarse language as befits none but a fish wife.

7. I Dislike your talking against me behind my back, and that everyday and almost every hour of the day; making my faults (real or supposed) the standing topic of your conversation.

8. I dislike your slandering me, laying to my charge things which you know are false. Such are (to go but a few days back) 'that I beat you,' which you told James Burges; that I rode to Kingswood with Sarah Ryan, which you told Sarah Rigby; and that I required you, when we were first married, never to sit in my presence without my leave, which you told Mrs. Lee, Mrs. Fry and several others, and stood to it before my face.

9. I dislike your common custom of saying things not true. To instance, only in two or three particulars. You told Mr. Ireland 'Mr Vazzilla learnt Spanish in a fortnight'. You told Mr. Fry 'Mrs. Ellison was the author as to my intrigue in Georgia'. You told Mrs. Ellison 'you never said any such thing; you never charged her with it'. You also told them 'that I had laid a plot to serve you as Susannah was served by the two elders'.

10. I dislike your extreme, immeasurable bitterness to all who endeavour to defend my character (as my brother, Joseph Jones, Clayton Carthy) breaking out even into foul, unmannerly language, such as ought not to defile a gentlewoman's lips, if she did not believe one world of the Bible.

And now Molly, what would anyone advise you to that has a real concern for your happiness? Certainly,

1. To show, read, touch those letters no more, if you did not restore them to their proper owner;

2. To allow me the command of my own house, with free leave to invite thither whom I please;

3. To allow me my liberty there, that anyone who will may come to me, without let or hindrance;

4. To let me go where I please and to whom I please without giving an account to any;

5. To assure me, you will take no more of my papers nor anything of mine without my consent;

6. To treat all the servants where you are (whether you like them or no) with courtesy and humanity and to speak (if you speak at all) to them, as well as others, with good-nature and good manners;

7. To speak no evil of me behind my back;

8. Never to accuse me falsely;

9. To be extremely cautious of saying anything that is not strictly true, both as to the matter and the manner; and

10. To avoid all bitterness of expression till you can avoid all bitterness of spirit.

These are the advises which I now give you in the fear of God, and in tender love to your soul. Nor can I give you a stronger proof that I am your affectionate husband,

John Wesley

Derek Prince in the Dungeon?

Derek Prince married two women and said only good things about his wives. What do you expect him to say? Bad things? Even if he had challenges with his wife, I would not expect him to talk about them or share them with the public. Would you? However, there are glimpses into the lonely "John the Baptist-in-the-dungeon experiences."

As many second wives do experience, Derek Prince's second wife, Ruth was not liked much by Derek Prince's family and some of his minister friends.

When Ruth, the second wife first arrived, Derek Prince's daughter, Johanne had a dream in which Ruth was pushing Derek in a wheelchair. They were in a building somewhere in New York when suddenly, Ruth pushed Derek violently down a great flight of stairs. All the while, Derek was screaming Johanne's name. When Johanne awoke, she was understandably horrified by the dream.

This dream was apparently confirmed by Don Basham's daughter who had a similar dream. These dreams did not help much to welcome Derek Prince's second wife!

Ruth, the second wife saw it as her duty to drive Derek Prince to the greatness she believed he was called to. Many people, however, remember her as a controlling woman. She was said to have regimented Derek Prince's life and schedule to the last possible detail. This made things difficult for Derek Prince and those around him.

When she and Derek visited the homes of family or friends, Ruth would announce exactly what Derek Prince would eat and when he would have his meals. Sometimes her instructions were sent in advance.

Once, Derek Prince went shopping with his wife and some friends. Derek Prince put some things in the shopping basket, which his wife did not want him to have. Ruth did not like it and immediately took the things away from Derek. In the end she became angry and reprimanded him so loudly that everyone in the shop heard her rebuking him. Some described her as "pretty raging and harsh".

When people called the house and asked for the man of God, they would be told he was sleeping or praying. Derek Prince, unaware of this, would wonder why people never called his house. The over-protectiveness of Ruth Prince led to a form of isolation.

His second wife was described by some people as "a frustrating combination of control and insecurity". Many of the people around Derek Prince believed that she actually hindered his ministry.

Someone's comment on Derek Prince's marriage was that the couple probably entered a vicious cycle, with Ruth trying to control Derek Prince's life to earn his love and Derek resenting the domination and withholding his love from Ruth.

Indeed, there were many good sides to Ruth and she did much to also help his ministry. The point I am trying to make is this. The picture of perfection presented by most ministers to the TV cameras is often not real. There are battles in the secret places, which must be fought and won. Insecurity, accusations and control must be understood for what they really are. You must be bold to fight the enemy in the dungeon. Don't let them cut off your head before your time.

Chapter 6

Various Types of Accusations

1.   Accusations by direct allegations

This is the easily recognized form of accusation. The voice of the accuser rings loud and clear through the statements that come forth. "You are proud and rude." "You are a drunkard." "You did not really want to marry me." "You prefer someone else." "You are in love with the pastor." "Can you not leave that young girl alone?"

These are examples of direct allegations voiced out boldly by the confident accuser. Notice this verse in which the servant directly accused his master.

Then he which had received the one talent came and said, Lord, I KNEW THEE THAT THOU ART AN HARD MAN, reaping where thou hast not sown, and gathering where thou hast not strawed:

Matthew 25:24

2.   Accusations by criticism

Criticism is making an opinion about someone's faults or bad qualities. It is a statement showing disapproval. Criticism is simply another form of accusation. Do not criticize people. Learn to speak good things and not evil. Do not be a person who constantly notices faults in people. Do not look out for bad qualities and point them out.

Pray for people, rather than accuse them! Notice how Aaron and Miriam accused Moses of marrying the wrong person.

And Miriam and Aaron spake against Moses because of the Ethiopian woman whom he had married: for he had married an Ethiopian woman.

Numbers 12:1

3.   Accusations by murmuring

Do all things without murmuring. Murmuring is when unfavourable comments and statements are made undertone. Murmurings are not intended to be heard by the accused but have the effect of poisoning anyone who hears them. Murmuring prevented the children of Israel from entering the Promised Land. God hears all our undertone comments and remarks! God is not deaf!

One day, a pastor was enjoying the music in the church as the choir ministered and his wife sat at his side. As he flowed happily with the music, his wife made a comment. At first, he thought he had not heard right.

He asked, "Pardon, what did you say?"

She whispered, "I said that I realize you cannot keep your eyes off her when she is singing in front."

Even though this remark was undertone it was powerful and loaded with venom. You can imagine the effect it had on someone who was just about to preach.

4.   Accusations by being present

Now there was a day when the sons of God came to present themselves before the Lord, and Satan came also among them.

Job 1:6

The very presence of certain people sends a message to all. The presence of police at a crime scene is a message that something criminal may have happened. The very presence of a uniformed officer always means something.

When Satan attended the meeting of the sons of God, his mind was full of accusations. His thoughts were classic accusations: "Does Job serve God for nothing?" In other words, Job was not a sincere servant of God. Satan was accusing Job of not really loving God. Certain people's minds are simply full of accusations. Their presence speaks volumes of suspicion.

5.   Accusations by being absent

The absence of certain people at meetings sends a loud message. This is why people speak of boycotting meetings. By boycotting meetings, they send a message, which is louder and stronger than, if they had come in person.

And it came to pass, when he was come to Jerusalem to meet the king, that the king said unto him, Wherefore wentest not thou with me, Mephibosheth?

2 Samuel 19:25

The absence of Mephibosheth at the time when King David fled was a message! The absence of Mephibosheth indicated he was not really on David's side.

One day, a pastor told me how his wife's absence on a ministry trip broke his heart. He had asked his wife to please come along with him but she refused.

Throughout the trip, the absence of his wife ministered an accusation to him! It weakened him and made it difficult for him to minister. His wife had refused to go with him, claiming that he was happier with other people.

She said to him, "You don't really want me around and I know it."

When he asked his wife again if she would come, her response was simple, "Are you going with your people? If you are going with those people of yours, I am not coming!" His heart was broken and he limped away to his programme.

6. Accusations by writing

And in the reign of Ahasuerus, in the beginning of his reign, WROTE THEY UNTO HIM AN ACCUSATION against the inhabitants of Judah and Jerusalem.

Ezra 4:6

This is the main method of accusation employed by journalists. They write stories which misrepresent events and remarks of honourable men and accuse them of much evil. A government usually becomes the enemy of the press as journalists heap up one accusation after another.

Many journalists are in search of a sensational story that will make the headlines. They need something spectacular that will make their newspapers sell. Unfortunately, honourable people fall victim to this quest for headline stories. Often, apologies for mistaken stories are small and insignificant. The damage is done already.

7. Accusations by suggestions and insinuations

An insinuation is an indirect suggestion that something unpleasant is true. The fact that you have not made a direct allegation does not mean that you are not accusing. Sometimes, these insinuations are more painful than direct allegations.

Instead of saying Jesus did not deserve such treatment, Judas suggested that they were being wasteful.

...To what purpose is this waste? For this ointment might have been sold for much, and given to the poor.

Matthew 26:8-9

Little comments can have far-reaching effects. One senior pastor sent a brother on a mission to help a nearby branch church become more established. This brother was excited about his new challenge. Unknown to him, the senior pastor's wife berated her husband for that move.

She had said to him, "You are sending away people's husbands so that you can have more time with their wives."

"What are you saying!" the pastor exclaimed.

But his wife insisted, "You are sending out this man to get him out of the way."

The pastor retorted, "How can you even think that way? How does your mind work?"

But the damage was done. The pastor was affected by this comment and decided not to send out the person. His very motives had been challenged to the core.

Naturally, it is the work of God which suffers. Many things are stopped through insinuations. That is the Jezebel spirit of controlling witchcraft.

8.   Accusations by sarcasm

Sarcasm is a way of using words that are the opposite of what you mean, in order to be unpleasant to somebody or to make fun of them. Sometimes, you may make a comment to someone but you mean the opposite. You may say, "thank you" but you mean "I hate you". You may say "God bless you" but you are actually wishing the person evil.

Naaman could see the greed in the eyes of Gehazi.

And Naaman said, Be content, take two talents. And he urged him...

2 Kings 5:23

One day, I sent a message to someone. My message was simple. I said, "Tell that guy that I said 'thank you'." However, the messenger refused to deliver the message. He knew that my "thank you" was loaded and did not really mean "thank you". What it actually meant was, "I have taken note of the evil, which you have done to me."

9. Accusations by silence

Many times silence speaks louder than words. The very silence of someone at a meeting can send a message. Not a word may be spoken but the silence of the committee member speaks volumes and says, "I don't enjoy working with you. You are a dictator. You always want to have your own way."

And Absalom spake unto his brother Amnon neither good nor bad: for Absalom hated Amnon, because he had forced his sister Tamar.

2 Samuel 13:22

10. Accusations by a continuous dropping

Continuous complaining that comes in little bits is a continuous dropping.

A continual dropping in a very rainy day and a contentious woman are alike.

Proverbs 27:15

Sometimes women feel that if they are too strong on an issue then they are being harsh.

Little hints about the same issue given as frequently as possible seem less confrontational. However, the greatest flood that I ever saw in my city did not come from a powerful tropical rainstorm but from a continuous dropping that lasted several hours. Watch out for the people who pester you with a continuous dropping.

11.   Accusations by a contentious woman

A contentious woman is an ill-natured cantankerous person. This kind of woman will "never agree, never give up, never give in, never say die, never flow, never yield, never bend, never say sorry, never bow, never back down, never concede defeat, never stop talking, never stop quarrelling, never stop arguing, never stop disagreeing and never stop opposing everything".

Accusatory women are contentious women who drive you away from their presence. It is better to be away from the presence of Satan, the accuser. This Scripture shows that the accuser can inhabit beautiful women and use them to wear out God's servant.

It is better to dwell in the wilderness, than with a contentious and an angry woman.

Proverbs 21:19

Truly, the wilderness would be a better home for you than the house you built.

It is better to dwell in a corner of the housetop, than with a brawling woman in a wide house.

Proverbs 21:9

John Wesley wrote to his wife and said, "I dislike not being safe in my own house."

12.   Accusations by re-describing events

It is a clever trick to re-describe and re-present events in a way that make them look evil. It is easy to re-tell a story in a way that darkens the event and makes things look negative. All you have to do is to highlight some areas and leave out some. This is what was done to Jesus. They re-presented His statements until He looked like a suicide bomber and an anarchist.

We heard him say, I will destroy this temple that is made with hands, and within three days I will build another made without hands.

Mark 14:58

And they began to accuse him, saying, We found this fellow perverting the nation, and forbidding to give tribute to Caesar, saying that he himself is Christ a King.

Luke 23:2

Watch out for people who re-tell events and make things look nasty, immoral and evil.

Chapter 7

Why Accusations Are Powerful

The Giant Trembles

I have often wondered why accusations have the effect they do. One day, I had the privilege of interacting with a great man of God. This man was a true spiritual giant. He had accomplished many things for the Lord. As he took us around his facilities, I was amazed at the things that God had accomplished through him. As we walked and drove around the various buildings, he made certain remarks, which made me sad. He seemed to be defending his reputation. He seemed to want to explain himself to us.

But I thought to myself, "Why is this man even bothering to clear his name?"

Then I remembered that a strange son of his had accused him of many evils. This disloyal pastor had maligned and defamed my honourable host. Much had been said in the media about the allegations against this man.

I realized that even this giant in the Lord had trembled under the sting of the accuser. I tell you, nothing can bring a great man to his knees like accusations! They need not be true! They just have to be accusations!

I want us to understand what makes accusations so powerful. Let us get to the bottom of this mystery. Let us find the source of accusatory power. When you understand why accusations are powerful, you will be able to overcome their effects.

The Source of Accusatory Power

1.   Accusations are powerful because they are all, basically, true.

For I know that in me (that is, in my flesh,) dwelleth no good thing...

Romans 7:18

An accusation is a dirty trick that capitalizes on the existing sinfulness and weakness of men. It points the finger at our weak spots and weak points.

Almost everything that we are accused of is true. The only thing I can liken accusations to, is to a cripple being made fun of by a person who walks normally. It is like pointing out to a paralyzed person that he is incapable and abnormal.

Making Fun of Cripples?

Accusing someone is like laughing at a deaf and dumb person and showing him how deficient he is in his hearing and his speech. How do you think the deaf and dumb person would feel when his deficiency is being demonstrated to others? That is what it is like when a sinner is being told that he is sinful.

The Bible already shows us how far from God we are. If you can imagine it, we are millions of years away from God's nature.

For as the heavens are higher than the earth, so are my ways higher than your ways, and my thoughts than your thoughts.

Isaiah 55:9

We are so far from true holiness and righteousness. Sin has separated us so far from God. It is only His mercy that brings us close.

Scripture Proves Our Sinfulness

The Bible teaches us that we are essentially sinners. There are enough Scriptures that declare us hopelessly and helplessly sinful. There is deep-seated evil in the heart of every human being and we know it. We need no one to confirm this well-established truth.

Notice all these Scriptures that confirm all that I am sharing:

...There is none righteous, no, not one.

Romans 3:10

For all have sinned and come short of the glory of God.

Romans 3:23

The heart is deceitful...and desperately wicked...

Jeremiah 17:9

God's Servants Confessed Their Sinfulness

Also, great men of God confessed that they were woefully sinful and inadequate when they came into the presence of God. Isaiah said,

...Woe is me! for I am undone; because I am a man of unclean lips, and I dwell in the midst of a people of unclean lips: for mine eyes have seen the King, the LORD of hosts.

Isaiah 6:5

Job found out that he was a very bad person when he came to the presence of the Lord. He actually abhorred himself when he realized what he was.

I have heard of thee by the hearing of the ear: but now mine eye seeth thee. Wherefore I abhor myself, and repent in dust and ashes.

Job 42:5-6

The great prophet, Daniel, also confesses how evil he was.

We have sinned, and have committed iniquity, and have done wickedly, and have rebelled, even by departing from thy precepts and from thy judgments:

Daniel 9:5

Also, the apostle Paul, at the end of his life described himself as the chief of sinners. He said,

...that Christ Jesus came into the world to save sinners, of whom I am chief.

1 Timothy 1:15

He called himself the chief of sinners in his very last letter. Paul called himself a wretched man who could not get rid of his sinfulness.

O wretched man that I am! who shall deliver me from the body of this death?

Romans 7:24

John Wesley Wondered

Interestingly, great men of God feel no sense of worthiness at the end of their lives. Notice what John Wesley said about himself at the end of his life. He said:

"I have been wandering up and down between fifty and sixty years, endeavoring, in my poor way, to do a little good to my fellow creatures; and now it is probable that there are but a few steps between me and death; and what have I to trust to for salvation? I can see nothing that I have done or suffered that will bear looking at. I have no other plea than this: I the chief of sinners am, but Jesus died for me."

Accuser, Watch Out for Yourself

That is why Jesus warned us to stay off judging other people. Whatever judgement you pass is a judgement on yourself.

Therefore you have no excuse, everyone of you who passes judgment, for in that which you judge another, you condemn yourself; for you who judge practice the same things"

Romans 2:1, NASB

Be careful when you accuse and judge someone. The Bible says that you are actually practising the same things over which you judge another. I believe that everything I have been accused about is true in principle. I actually feel that they are true and I endeavour to confess my sins everyday.

If someone accused me of stealing the church's money, I would believe it is true. Perhaps I have taken money that I was not aware of? Perhaps I have mismanaged some of God's money? Perhaps I have wasted the church's money? Perhaps I have overpaid myself? Perhaps I have enjoyed luxuries that were not right? How could I tell? In all honesty, my sinful nature is real and I cannot deny it even though I am a preacher. That is why I confess my sins everyday.

If someone accused me of adultery, I would believe that it is true and I would confess my sins. I cannot deny much because Scripture says that if you look on a woman to lust after her you have already committed adultery (Matthew 5:28). I must have done this many times over and I always pray for mercy for my soul.

If somebody accused me of witchcraft, I would agree because rebellion is as the sin of witchcraft (1 Samuel 15:23). I must have been rebellious against the Lord many times.

We must be like Daniel who confessed these terrible sins in the first person. He believed he had committed them. His thinking was not, "I am greatly loved by the Lord. I am a great prophet of God." His thoughts were more, "I am a sinner who needs the grace of God." Notice his prayer:

And I prayed unto the LORD my God, and made my confession, and said, O Lord, the great and dreadful God, keeping the covenant and mercy to them that love him, and to them that keep his commandments;

We have sinned, and have committed iniquity, and have done wickedly, and have rebelled, even by departing from thy precepts and from thy judgments:

Neither have we hearkened unto thy servants the prophets, which spake in thy name to our kings, our princes, and our fathers, and to all the people of the land.

O Lord, righteousness belongeth unto thee, but unto us confusion of faces...

Daniel 9:4-7

The Power of Accusation Lies in the Power of Truth

It is the truth of this sinful nature that gives power to accusations. No matter how you deny an accusation, it will have an effect on you. No matter how untrue an accusation is, it will damage you. You will think about what was said and you will be disturbed. You will be uncertain about whether the allegations are really true or not. I know of no other weapon that can administer confusion to your life in such large doses.

2.   Accusations are powerful because they stereotype you.

It is because these accusations match you so perfectly with a known stereotype that they have such power over you. Accusations tend to categorize or stereotype a person.

These stereotypes are associated with a number of evils. These stereotypes have been proven guilty over and over. Statistics show that these stereotypes do the things they are accused of.

A woman who becomes a stepmother by virtue of her husband's past frolicking is matched perfectly with the stereotype of the wicked and selfish stepmother. No matter what she does and how much she cares for her stepchildren, she matches too well with the wicked stepmother stereotype. She will probably live her entire life under that shadow.

The stereotype of an unmarried, young, pretty lady in the church is that of a husband seeker. It is very easy to believe that every single young lady in the church is simply seeking a husband. No matter how spiritual she looks, it is believed that she is looking for a husband. She fits perfectly into the husband-seeking stereotype. Such a person may be accused of even hoping to snatch somebody's husband.

A stereotype of men is the adulterous husband who cannot stick to his wife. Therefore, when a married man with a grumpy out-of-shape wife is accused of adultery, he fits perfectly into the adulterous husband stereotype. Matching a man to this stereotype is very powerful because such a man is a perfect match for that category.

I remember a single unattached lady who was the worship leader in her church. She led the praises and she loved to worship God. She and many other sisters in the church had enjoyed a good relationship with their pastor.

One day, out of the blue, the pastor's wife came up to her and said, "You can never have my husband. No matter what you do you will never have him! I want you to know that I have three children with him and he will never marry you!"

"I just want you to know," she concluded.

The worship leader was shocked, to say the least. She did not understand what was happening.

The pastor found himself in a very uncomfortable situation, having to balance the relationship between his wife and his worship leader. To say the least, the relationships became awkward and permanently disrupted.

This sudden accusation by the pastor's wife had tremendous power because the worship leader fitted into the "single lady, husband-seeking" stereotype whilst the pastor also fitted the "adulterous husband with a grumpy wife" stereotype.

It is because these accusations match you so perfectly with a known stereotype that they have such power over you.

3.   Accusations have power because they thrive on the power of deception.

If what the accuser of the brethren says is the right thing, then judgement must be meted out to us. Somehow, God does not pass the judgements that correspond to all these accusations. If most accusations were followed up, many of the accused people would have to be put to death and sent to Hell.

Somehow, the accusations are not valid. We have been declared not guilty to all charges, allegations and accusations because of the blood of Jesus. The blood of Jesus and the mercy of God have changed the equation and rendered the accusations useless. Satan knows this but he still intimidates us and harasses us with accusations, guilt and fear until we are confused. He fights us with so much confusion that we do not know whether we are good or bad!

Because of the blood of Jesus we are forgiven and we are free. God actually loves us and really likes us though it is difficult to believe sometimes. He wants us to be with Him and He has a deep, passionate and warm feeling for us. Because of accusations, I sometimes find it difficult to believe that God loves me. I feel sinful and I know the reality of sin in me. Satan thrives on these feelings and condemns me constantly. But we shall overcome the accuser of the brethren in Jesus' name.

4. Accusations have an effect because Satan's spiritual power is behind every accusation.

Satan is a spirit and he works spiritually through the weapon of accusation. Satan intimidates and harasses God's servants. His aim is to remove you from the ministry and stop you from doing the good things God has called you to. I assure you, many of the bad thoughts that come to your mind are from the devil.

Resist the power behind the accusations and recognize that a spiritual force is working against you. You are a good person and God believes in you!

Chapter 8

Other Works of the Accuser

The devil attacks a Christian in several forms. Moses and our Lord Jesus experienced the onslaught of the devil in the form of an accuser. They sustained relentless attacks in the form of complaints and accusations.

The anointing upon Moses was of the highest order. God used Moses to build His people into a great nation.

Jesus was perfect and yet He was accused until His life was snuffed out.

Everyone who takes up the call of God is truly an honourable person. In spite of what people say, very few people ever opt for the service of the Lord. Very few people have the faith to obey the call to ministry. In spite of this great effort, ministers are vilified and denigrated constantly. Every attempt to serve God in ministry is a great and honourable effort.

Yet, why are ministers constantly accused of various evils? Ask Moses and ask the Lord Jesus Christ. Moses finally erred in ministry when he responded to the complaints of the people. He was perfect in obedience to the Lord, fulfilling every detailed command that God gave him. It was the incessant complaints of the children of Israel that pushed him to the brink. Accusations push people to do things that they would not have done.

1.   The accuser opposes us.

When our first church was being built, Satan attacked us in the form of an antagonistic man. He opposed everything we did in the community. He fought against us and drew the government, the community and the media against me. I was amazed at how kind gestures had turned into the most complicated persecution of my ministry.

But the prince of the kingdom of Persia withstood me one and twenty days...

Daniel 10:13

2.   The accuser tried to kill me.

This is another thing to expect from the accuser of the brethren. He will try to kill you. And I mean this literally. Satan would love to eliminate you through any possible means. He would love to drown you, poison you, strangulate you, kill you in an accident, or inflict a disease on a part of your body.

Do not take this lightly. Every minister must take precautions to keep yourself alive. Give no place to the devil. I have been in planes that almost crashed. I have been in cars that somersaulted. I have been inflicted with disease that almost killed me. In all these, I see the accuser trying his hand as a murderer.

The thief cometh not, but for to steal, and TO KILL...

John 10:10

3.   The accuser tempts us.

Then was Jesus led up of the Spirit into the wilderness to be TEMPTED OF THE DEVIL.

Matthew 4:1

I have been tempted by the devil in many different ways. I am sure you would like to know what temptations I have had. Well, I cannot give the details here but I have been tempted in almost everything you can imagine. One day, the Lord told me that I had overcome a season of temptation. I was surprised to hear this but He explained that I had experienced a season of temptation, which I had survived.

Three Temptations of Ministers

Every minister will experience three temptations. Jesus experienced them and so will you. You will experience temptations with the flesh. Jesus was tempted to turn stones into bread to satisfy His flesh.

You will experience temptations to misuse your authority and power. Jesus was tempted to use His power to jump off a cliff and call for angels.

Finally, you will be tempted to use the short cut of ministry. Satan offered Jesus a fast way to win the world. "Bow down and worship me," he said, "and the whole world will be given back to you." This short cut says, "Go the quick way where there is no pain, no sacrifice and nothing hard." Fortunately, Jesus did not fall to any of these temptations.

4.   The accuser wanted me to be worldly.

Satan is the prince of this world. He is the spirit behind the worldly trends and fashions. As Christians become more worldly, they are playing into the hands of the prince of the world. Ministers are constantly under pressure to do and say things that the prince of the world desires.

Ministers are pressurized into becoming worldly motivational speakers rather than preachers of divine secrets. In addition, many ministers have become givers of good advice about the felt needs of their members. This is worldliness in the pulpit. This is a departure from the preaching of divine mysteries, which Christ has given to us.

Love not the world, neither the things that are in the world. If any man love the world, the love of the Father is not in him.

For all that is in the world, the lust of the flesh, and the lust of the eyes, and the pride of life, is not of the Father, but is of the world.

1 John 2: 15,16

5.   The accuser wants to make us unclean.

The devil wants to make you dirty. His aim is to bring all manner of filthiness into your life. All kinds of lustful and immoral activities will make you dirty. Certain films, pornography, secular music and profanity are Satan's tools to dirty your life. The devil is often called an unclean spirit (Mark 1:23).

6.   The accuser will influence you through the air.

...ye walked according to the course of this world, according to the PRINCE OF THE POWER OF THE AIR, the spirit that now worketh in the children of disobedience:

Ephesians 2:2

The accuser has possessed the airwaves of every nation. As the prince of the power of the air, he channels much evil through the radio, television and internet. This is why it is important for Christians to gain access and control of the airwaves of their countries.

You must fight to go on air and join the battle in the atmosphere. Elections are won and lost in the air. The morality of a nation is destroyed in the air. But souls are also won through the airwaves.

7.   The accuser will try to make you worthless.

The name Belial means worthlessness. Satan is trying to make your ministry worthless. He wants to make you personally worthless!

> **...by means of a whorish woman a man is brought to a piece of bread...**
>
> **Proverbs 6:26**

Satan wants to reduce you to the lowest possible level in this life. That is the spirit of poverty, uselessness and worthlessness. Be delivered in Jesus' name!

8.   The accuser will try to rule you.

Satan is the ruler of darkness. When you walk in sin and darkness, you are walking into his hands.

Stay away from sin; stay away from that realm and stay close to the light.

> **For we wrestle...against the RULERS OF THE DARKNESS of this world...**
>
> **Ephesians 6:12**

9.   The accuser will deceive you.

Satan's strength towards you is deception. Persistent lying and deceptive tricks have made him the master deceiver of all time. He will try to deceive you into believing many things that are not so. Most of our difficulties come from our delusions. Most of our sorrows are because of erroneous things that we have believed.

If Satan is able to deceive the whole world then you must constantly ask yourself what current delusion you may have.

...that old serpent, called the Devil, and Satan, WHICH DECEIVETH the whole world...

Revelation 12:9

10.   The accuser will fight with you.

Be sober, be vigilant; because YOUR ADVERSARY THE DEVIL, as a roaring lion, walketh about, seeking whom he may devour:

1 Peter 5:8

Expect the fight of your life as you step into ministry! You will be fighting until your very last day. Intelligent demons, wicked spirits and wrestling powers will engage you until you lie down in the grave.

You need supernatural wisdom and closeness to God to survive. It is not about power. It is about fighting a liar and a clever deceiver. "Adversary" means a challenger, an opponent, an enemy and an antagonist. You can expect to be antagonized and challenged throughout your entire ministry. That is one of the key works of the accuser in the midst of the brethren.

Chapter 9

How to Silence the Accuser

There are many benefits of fighting the accuser in your life. There are also many different ways you must take on this vicious enemy.

1. Prayer

...seeing he ever liveth to make intercession for them.

Hebrews 7:25

Prayer is the way to fight the spiritual power that is behind accusation. Jesus ever liveth to make intercession for us.

The intercession of Christ is directly countering the accusations of Satan. Prayer is the opposite of accusation. As Satan points out our weaknesses, Jesus is presenting His blood before the throne, explaining why we must not be condemned.

Join your prayer with the prayers of Christ and counteract the force of accusation against your ministry. Set up prayer warriors to intercede for you constantly so that the power of the accuser will be broken.

2. Open Confrontation

They say unto him, Master, this woman was taken in adultery, in the very act.

Now Moses in the law commanded us, that such should be stoned: but what sayest thou?

This they said, tempting him, that they might have to accuse him. But Jesus stooped down, and with his finger wrote on the ground, as though he heard them not.

So when they continued asking him, he lifted up himself, and said unto them, He that is without sin among you, LET HIM FIRST CAST A STONE AT HER.

And again he stooped down, and wrote on the ground.

And they which heard it, being convicted by their own conscience, went out one by one, beginning at the eldest, even unto the last: and Jesus was left alone, and the woman standing in the midst.

When Jesus had lifted up himself, and saw none but the woman, he said unto her, Woman, where are those thine accusers? hath no man condemned thee?

She said, No man, Lord. And Jesus said unto her, Neither do I condemn thee: go, and sin no more.

John 8:4-11

Jesus introduced the accused to the accusers and He asked the accusers to implement the judgement of their allegations. He wanted them to carry their accusation to its logical conclusion.

Many accusers love to hide behind the curtain and shoot their arrows. They do not want anybody to know what they think or say. Openly confronting accusers can be a good way to free yourself. Years ago, I confronted a brother who was accusing me of not being called to the ministry.

I said to him, "If I am not called, why are you in this church? If I am not anointed, why do you come to this church every week?"

This fellow was shocked at the confrontation. You see, accusers love to hide behind the scenes and say things about you. When they see you, they phlegmatise and flow as though everything is normal. You would never know what is said behind your back by the smiles and jolly friendship they exhibit.

3. Teaching

Teaching is a powerful tool that deals a deadly blow to ignorance and deception. Jesus responded to several of the accusations against Him with teachings. Let me give you a few examples. You can hold a large team together when you teach them. Most leaders just warn their followers to desist from certain things. But teaching is more powerful than issuing warnings.

a.   Jesus was accused of not letting His pastors fast so He taught on the new wineskins.

The disciples of John and of the Pharisees were fasting. Then they came and said to Him, "WHY DO THE DISCIPLES OF JOHN AND OF THE PHARISEES FAST, but Your disciples do not fast?"

And Jesus said to them, "Can the friends of the bridegroom fast while the bridegroom is with them? As long as they have the bridegroom with them they cannot fast.

But the days will come when the bridegroom will be taken away from them, and then they will fast in those days.

No one sews a piece of unshrunk cloth on an old garment; or else the new piece pulls away from the old, and the tear is made worse.

And no one puts new wine into old wineskins; or else the new wine bursts the wineskins, the wine is spilled, and the wineskins are ruined. But new wine must be put into new wineskins."

Mark 2:18-22, NKJV

b.   When Jesus was accused of not washing His hands, He gave a teaching that addressed the issue.

Then the Pharisees and scribes asked him, WHY WALK NOT THY DISCIPLES ACCORDING TO THE TRADITION OF THE ELDERS, but eat bread with unwashen hands?

He answered and said unto them, Well hath Esaias prophesied of you hypocrites, as it is written, This people honoureth me with their lips, but their heart is far from me.

Howbeit in vain do they worship me, teaching for doctrines the commandments of men.

Mark 7:5-7

c.   Jesus was also accused of being a mere carpenter posing as a man of God. In response to this, He gave a teaching on how a prophet is not accepted in his own home.

IS NOT THIS THE CARPENTER, the son of Mary, the brother of James, and Joses, and of Juda, and Simon? and are not his sisters here with us? And they were offended at him.

But Jesus said unto them, A prophet is not without honour, but in his own country, and among his own kin, and in his own house.

Mark 6:3-4

d.   Jesus was accused of eating with sinners so He taught on evangelism.

And when the scribes and Pharisees saw him eat with publicans and sinners, they said unto his disciples, HOW IS IT THAT HE EATETH AND DRINKETH WITH PUBLICANS AND SINNERS?

When Jesus heard it, he saith unto them, They that are whole have no need of the physician, but they that are sick: I came not to call the righteous, but sinners to repentance.

Mark 2:16-17

4. Common-Sense Logic

One of the ways to counteract accusations is to use common sense to make nonsense of the accusations. You must learn to use logical arguments that destroy the foundation of the accusation.

Jesus did this often. When Jesus was accused of having political aspirations, He answered with logical arguments. He said, "If my kingdom were of this world, my servants would fight." Is it not logical for a king to have his army fight for him?

Jesus answered, my kingdom is not of this world: if my kingdom were of this world, then would my servants fight, that I should not be delivered to the Jews: but now is my kingdom not from hence.

John 18:36

I use those arguments a lot. I ask questions like, "If I was after money, would I not practise medicine?"

"If all I wanted were nice cars and a nice house, why would I choose to be a priest? Could I not just practise medicine in America and earn lots of money for myself?"

Common sense alone will dispel numerous baseless accusations from the mouths of hateful enemies of the cross.

5. Agree with Your Accusers

AGREE WITH THINE ADVERSARY QUICKLY, whiles thou art in the way with him; lest at any time the adversary deliver thee to the judge, and the judge deliver thee to the officer, and thou be cast into prison.

Matthew 5:25

The Bible teaches us to agree with our accusers. The truth is that we are guilty of almost everything we are accused of. Agreeing with your accuser can be a powerful strategy to silence the accuser. Jesus used this method when He was on trial. By saying, "I am" and "thou sayest" He agreed with His accusers. It was now up to them to follow their prosecution to its logical conclusion.

Jesus Agreed with His Accusers

AND JESUS SAID, I AM: and ye shall see the Son of man sitting on the right hand of power, and coming in the clouds of heaven.

Mark 14:62

And Pilate asked him, Art thou the King of the Jews? AND HE ANSWERING SAID UNTO HIM, THOU SAYEST IT.

Mark 15:2

6. Silence

Not answering accusations that are levelled against you is yet another way to silence the accuser. Journalists hate to hear the wise words, "I have no comment to make at this time." Journalists love to interview controversial figures. Each time a public figure is interviewed, he says something they can hold onto and accuse him of. One of the best policies for ministers is to make no comments and to give no interviews about anything for any reason!

Jesus saw no reason why He should answer questions. All He had to say was what He had preached. They could get the tapes if they wanted to, and hear it for themselves. Pastors must learn from the Saviour.

People questioning you in a hostile environment is not going to give a true picture of who you are. People should listen to what you preach and make up their minds. Hopefully, they will be saved and convicted by the time they have heard your message.

Jesus answered him, I spake openly to the world; I ever taught in the synagogue, and in the temple, whither the Jews always resort; and in secret have I said nothing.

WHY ASKEST THOU ME? ASK THEM WHICH HEARD ME, what I have said unto them: behold, they know what I said.

John 18:20-21

Jesus used this strategy when He met with Pilate. Pilate could not believe that Jesus would not speak to him. If Jesus did not want to speak to Pilate, how come pastors yearn to be interviewed by the secular world? Why are we so different from our Saviour?

And went again into the judgment hall, and saith unto Jesus, Whence art thou? But JESUS GAVE HIM NO ANSWER.

Then saith Pilate unto him, SPEAKEST THOU NOT UNTO ME? knowest thou not that I have power to crucify thee, and have power to release thee?

Jesus answered, Thou couldest have no power at all against me, except it were given thee from above: therefore he that delivered me unto thee hath the greater sin.

John 19:9-11

You must not be ashamed of the accusations that are levelled against you. Our Father has given us a cup to drink. Shall we not drink it? Allow the accusers to go ahead and paint you in whatever colours they wish. God is judge and He will vindicate you. There is nothing that anyone can do to prevent you from fulfilling God's call. Like Jesus told Pilate, no one can have power over your life and ministry except God gives it. God is in control and His hand is over all of us.

Chapter 10

A Warning to Accusers

P salm 109 contains a prophetic prayer against accusers. In the twentieth verse, the Psalmist summarizes his desire that all he has said should be the reward of his accusers.

Let this be the reward of my accusers from the LORD, and of those who speak evil against my soul.

Psalm 109:20

This is one of the most terrible and detailed curses you will find anywhere in the Bible. It ranges from the present life to the future of all descendants of the accuser. It is a sober warning to us all to leave God's servants alone. God will judge them.

There is no point in you invoking Psalm 109 against your life. Read it for yourself and decide to stay away from the reward of accusations.

Psalm 109

O God of my praise, Do not be silent!

For they have opened the wicked and deceitful mouth against me; They have spoken against me with a lying tongue.

They have also surrounded me with words of hatred, And fought against me without cause.

IN RETURN FOR MY LOVE THEY ACT AS MY ACCUSERS; But I am in prayer.

Thus they have repaid me evil for good And hatred for my love.

Appoint a wicked man over him, AND LET AN ACCUSER STAND AT HIS RIGHT HAND.

When he is judged, let him come forth guilty, And let his prayer become sin.

Let his days be few; Let another take his office.

Let his children be fatherless And his wife a widow.

Let his children wander about and beg; And let them seek sustenance far from their ruined homes.

Let the creditor seize all that he has, And let strangers plunder the product of his labor.

Let there be none to extend lovingkindness to him, Nor any to be gracious to his fatherless children.

Let his posterity be cut off; In a following generation let their name be blotted out.

Let the iniquity of his fathers be remembered before the LORD, And do not let the sin of his mother be blotted out.

Let them be before the LORD continually, That He may cut off their memory from the earth;

Because he did not remember to show lovingkindness, But persecuted the afflicted and needy man, And the despondent in heart, to put them to death.

He also loved cursing, so it came to him; And he did not delight in blessing, so it was far from him.

But he clothed himself with cursing as with his garment, And it entered into his body like water And like oil into his bones.

Let it be to him as a garment with which he covers himself, And for a belt with which he constantly girds himself.

LET THIS BE THE REWARD OF MY ACCUSERS FROM THE LORD, AND OF THOSE WHO SPEAK EVIL AGAINST MY SOUL.

Psalm 109:1-20, NASB

To the making of many books there is no end. May this book bless your ministry. Amen.

Other Best-Selling Books by Dag Heward-Mills:

*Loyalty and Disloyalty

Leaders and Loyalty

Transform Your Pastoral Ministry

The Art of Leadership

Model Marriage

Church Planting

*The Megachurch

*Lay People and the Ministry

*These titles are also available in Spanish and French. Information about
other foreign translations of some of the titles above may be obtained by
writing to our address.